# WHAT'S WRONG WITH WESTERN MISSIONS?

## THE PERSPECTIVE OF A LOCAL BELIEVER

**Translation by Michael and Olga Cantrell**

## KANAT YESMAGAMBETOV

AMBASSADOR INTERNATIONAL
GREENVILLE, SOUTH CAROLINA & BELFAST, NORTHERN IRELAND

www.ambassador-international.com

# What's Wrong with Western Missions?

The Perspective of a Local Believer
©2021 by Kanat Yesmagambetov

ISBN: 978-1-64960-106-3
eISBN: 978-1-64960-156-8

Cover Design by Christopher Jackson
Interior Typesetting by Dentelle Design
Digital Edition by Anna Riebe Raats

AMBASSADOR INTERNATIONAL
Emerald House
411 University Ridge, Suite B14
Greenville, SC 29601, USA
www.ambassador-international.com

AMBASSADOR BOOKS
The Mount
2 Woodstock Link
Belfast, BT6 8DD, Northern Ireland, UK
www.ambassadormedia.co.uk

*The colophon is a trademark of Ambassador, a Christian publishing company.*

*Dedicated to those far from home, deep in the mountains of China, on the steppes of Kazakhstan, and in the deserts of the Middle East, far away from the beaches of San Diego, family members in Texas, and the prices of Walmart. Whom we call missionaries.*

# WHAT'S WRONG WITH WESTERN MISSIONS?

Kanat, like a weeping prophet, speaks difficult truths to we who are stubborn in our refusal to hear. But praise unto Jesus, the Spirit of the living God gives us ears to hear, even as He has given Kanat the words to write. Prepare to be bruised, challenged, enlightened. Then let us labor together to ensure our Gospel methods match our Gospel message. Souls, both of those who speak and of those who hear, depend on it.

**DR. R.C. SPROUL, JR.**, Sinner saved by grace

*What is Wrong with Western Missions*: Don't be misled by the title. This is not a rant from a disgruntled Central Asian church leader. Instead, this is the heart of a first-generation, Central Asian follower of Christ who desires to see his people encounter the love and power of Jesus' kingdom. This is a must-read for anyone wanting to do cross-cultural, contextualized ministry focused on empowering local leaders. One of the first books ever written by a Central Asian believer for Western cross-cultural workers, it shows his love for those who brought the Good News to his people while at the same time offering necessary advice on how to do the task better.

**S.H.**, Western-born, Cross-Cultural Worker in Central Asia since 1998

Those of us who are concerned with the Great Commission of our Lord Jesus Christ being obediently carried out to the last frontiers will find this book very helpful. Mission is not black and white; it has many shades. And those shades vary from continent to continent, from race to race, and from culture to culture. We can learn Central Asian shade in this book. Kazakhs, Uzbeks, Kyrgyzes, Uighurs, Karakalpaks, Tatars, and other Turkic peoples are still extremely unreached. We still have to pour many efforts, say many prayers, spend much money, and send many missionaries. And before we send, we have to read this book. Readers may find the book very easy and funny to read. It is true. But it is deep inside. It contains more than ten years of experience on the field. Central Asian field. Physical, emotional, and spiritual experience. Hopefully, after reading this book, we will be more prepared to do the work and be wiser in our approaches. I highly recommend this book.

**DR. ALI ZHANKABAYEV**, DTL, Professor of Ministry and Leadership and Central Asia Regional Director at Grace School of Theology

# TABLE OF CONTENTS

# A NOTE FROM THE TRANSLATORS

MY WIFE, OLGA, AND I are thankful for the opportunity to work on this book. We are an international couple (I am American; Olga is Russian), and the themes and experiences related here are very familiar to us. Sadly, I have made my share of mistakes, some of which mirror situations of which Kanat writes. It's good and healthy to address missteps and hurtful acts which are done even with the very best of intentions.

This book is written in love, with a desire to give a perspective that is lacking in Christian literature: a local believer's view of missions. Almost all books on missions are written by missionaries or by people who study missions and yet remain in their home culture. It's good and appropriate to add this voice, with the hope that others will have a deeper understanding of the complex relationship between foreign and local believers.

From our experience, many missionaries these days arrive in the field with little understanding and respect for the history and heritage of the people they serve. Local believers suffer for it because they must submit to those who don't comprehend the richness of their home culture. We hope this book will prompt people to think more deeply about these issues as they prepare and count the cost before committing to missions. Western missionaries (really, *all* missionaries) would do well to consider the perspectives and experiences of local believers as they enter into partnership.

This is done for the glory of God and for the unity of the saints.

MICHAEL AND OLGA CANTRELL
St. Petersburg, Russia

# ACKNOWLEDGMENTS

ECCLESIASTES 4:9-1 SAYS, "TWO ARE better than one, because they have a good return for their labor: If either of them falls down, one can help the other up. But pity anyone who falls and has no one to help them up."

Books are written in private to be seen by many others. In order to accomplish this, one needs friends and colleagues to help make one's dreams come true.

I am grateful to Michael and Olga Cantrell for their amazing translation from Russian into English. For several months, we went through the entire book chapter by chapter: arguing, proposing ideas, and making decisions. Later, they provided assistance in finding publishers. And they did all this selflessly. I am indebted to them.

My thanks to Ali Zhankabayev and Aydar Yermekbaev for their support and valuable advice.

I am grateful to Alexander Knyazkov and The Eurasia Gateway Foundation for financial support in publishing the book.

My thanks to Sam Lowry and the entire Ambassador International team for their courage to publish what others were reluctant to bring to print.

Many thanks go to my beautiful wife, Dinara, and our three children—Daria, Saniyar, and Didar—for their love and understanding and for helping me balance ministry, writing, and my daily profession.

I thank the Father, the Son, and Holy Spirit for the courage and strength to say what should be said, as it should be said, despite the fact that some readers may like it and others may not.

# PREFACE

ONCE, I WAS INVITED TO speak at a conference near Minneapolis, but I was deprived of the microphone. Today, I have the opportunity to take it up.

I hope to be useful. I am not writing this book to offend anyone—not mission organizations, individual missionaries, or church leaders. I surely believe in the sincere desire of many to extend the Kingdom of God to unreached peoples. I believe that the most valuable assistance the West can offer to third-world countries (as first-world countries call them) is not "promotion of democracy," large grants, or profitable loans, but simple and faithful missionaries who are willing to exchange the green streets of Portland for the broken roads of Kabul, pickups for public transport, and the title of vice president for the dreaded word "missionary."

Christ is the One needed by the nations.

I was struck by an interview by Grigory Chkhartishvili[1] with one of the richest people in Russia, Mikhail Khodorkovsky. At the time of the interview, Khodorkovsky had spent five years in prison.[2] He said, "If there is no God, and all of our life is but an instant on the way from dust to dust, then what's the point of everything? What's the point of our dreams, our aspirations, our sufferings? What's the point of knowing? What's the point of loving? When it comes right down to it, what is the point of living?"[3]

---

1   Григорий Чхартишвили – Russian writer, scholar and translator, specializing in Japanese culture, working under the pen name Boris Akunin.

2   A Russian businessman, an oligarch—his report on corruption led to an open confrontation with Russian president Vladimir Putin and his subsequent trial and imprisonment regarding the oil company Yukos.

3   Robert Amsterdam, "Esquire Interview with Mikhail Khodorkovsky, Part 3 of 5," RobertAmsterdam.com, October 8, 2008. https://robertamsterdam.com/esquire_interview_with_mikhail_khodorkovsky_part_3_of_5.

Many unbelievers who live in the post-Soviet space understand that there must be meaning to life. Therefore, the work of missionaries—with whatever criticism and, often. indifference they may face—is invaluable.

I think this book will be useful for those who prepare for the field and those who are already there, as well as for those who send them—heads of missions and churches who direct the work of their missionaries. It will be useful—not only to those who go to Central Asia (where I live) but also to Poland, Mozambique, Bulgaria, Venezuela, and Belarus. We locals—black and yellow, quiet and rambunctious, educated and uneducated—are so different from one another; but as it turns out, the problems are often the same. When I share the ideas from this book at conferences, seminars, and leadership schools, local ministers support me.

The book will likely make some angry, as it did at a conference in Pattaya, Thailand, for those who minister to Muslims. One Western missionary was outraged by my words, while another, an African, cheered happily. Some in the West may say, "And this is the thanks we get for all that we have done for them." But others may be listening to a voice, one that possibly personifies thousands of voices in many languages and dialects. Kazakhs have a proverb: "A friend makes you cry, and an enemy makes you laugh."

My name is Kanat. I am a Kazakh, and I live in Kazakhstan. My parents are a retired police officer and a housewife. I received Christ eighteen years ago at the age of twenty-four. Of these, almost ten were served with a local branch of a large North American mission. I began as an assistant teacher and later served as Director of Church Planting of Russian-speaking churches. I studied at a leadership training institute and received a master's degree at a non-accredited seminary.

This is the story of my mission from my perspective, yet it resembles the stories of many others. This is not scientific research, but even such a serious science as statistics does not always tell the truth. (According to statistics, the number of "decisions for Jesus" in Ukraine is three times the population of Ukraine.) And subjective viewpoints are quite often confirmed by eyewitnesses.

The situations are real; only, the names have been changed.

CHAPTER 1

# BEGINNINGS

AS A CHILD, MY GRANDMOTHER taught me to pray at bedtime. I prayed loudly, trying to imitate the muezzins.[4] Once, after listening to my prayers, my grandmother said, "Someday, you will become a mullah."[5] And it turned out that I really did become a minister. Though, back then, I did not know the One Whom I would serve.

Despite all the prayers, I was not interested in religion. After graduation from high school, I decided to achieve something in life, to become someone successful, famous. To this end, I decided to go to the capital of our country and enroll in the Institute of Cinematography, yet at the same time, I didn't care exactly what I would study as long as I was accepted. Therefore, I applied to be an animator, an actor, a director, or a writer. But I couldn't draw; I had poor knowledge of the Kazakh language (a requirement for an actor); and I'd never written a script. When I came for an interview at the Kazakh Drama Theater, the great director Azerbaijan Mambetov[6] met me at the door and asked, "Do you know who Antonioni is?" I did not know. He said, "What can I talk to you about?"

Still, they accepted me to study documentary filmmaking. First thing, I went to the library and researched Michelangelo Antonioni.[7] It was there at the institute that I began to read a lot: Salinger, Kafka, Proust, Dostoevsky,

---

4    In Islam, a servant of the mosque calling Muslims to prayer
5    A minister in the mosque and head of a Muslim community
6    Soviet Kazakh director of theater and cinema, National Artist of the USSR (1976), National Hero of Kazakhstan (2000)
7    Italian film director and screenwriter, a classic of European cinema, who was called "the poet of alienation and loneliness"

Camus. It was then that I began to gradually go crazy. Why? Well, because many of them said life makes no sense: one day, you will turn into a cockroach; they will throw an apple at you; it will get stuck and begin to rot. Books posed questions but gave no answers. In addition to reading books, I loved to walk and look at the sky. For long stretches of time, I would stop in the middle of the sidewalk and look up. Sometimes, I stood next to someone's house, car, or fence, and then people would come out and chase me off.

In the third year, I became depressed. I stopped attending classes, did not eat, lay for hours in bed. After a few months of such a fruitful pastime, I decided to return to my hometown, Semipalatinsk,[8] a small town in East Kazakhstan.

Ah, but I have not told you about my country. It is called Kazakhstan. When I first came many years later to the city of Brooklyn Park, Minnesota, in the United States, I attended a Sunday service, and a church member asked me, "Where are you from?"

I said, "Kazakhstan."

"Pakistan?"

"No, Kazakhstan."

"Afghanistan?"

I soon realized that for most Americans, all of the "Stan" countries are somewhere between Pakistan and Afghanistan. To the surprise of many, Kazakhstan is not there. My country is located between the polar bear and the red dragon, between two super powers: Russia and China. It covers a huge territory, the ninth largest in the world. My American friends describe the size of Kazakhstan to their relatives by saying that the country is three times larger than Texas (although it is four times larger, to be exact) with a small population of only seventeen million; we say that there are as many of us as live in Moscow. It is a country of infinite steppe[9]: you can drive a thousand kilometers by car and not see a single city.

---

8   One hundred thirty kilometers from the city, the largest nuclear test site of the USSR
9   A large area of flat unforested grassland

After returning home, and of course without graduating from university, I decided to do two things: stop reading books and start drinking vodka. Later, I heard many testimonies of how people in search of God had quit drinking, smoking, and leading an immoral lifestyle. On the contrary, in my search, I began to drink (before that I had never drunk anything stronger than koumiss[10]) and also began to look for meetings with the beautiful half of humanity.

After a couple of years of such a life, my close friend Ruslan said, "Come with me to the English club."

"What for? I don't know English."

"Nobody there knows English."

"Well, okay."

So, we came to the English club. When everyone laughed, we laughed; when everyone was silent, we were silent. In this way, each of us hid his ignorance of English. We sang songs, played games. Once, an American gave Ruslan a Bible, and I asked, "Why don't you give me a Bible?"

"Will you read it?"

"Of course."

So, the Bible came to me; and for the first time in many years, I began to read. When people ask who led me to the Lord, I find it difficult to answer because the Bible led me to God. Nobody told me the Gospel; no one witnessed to me. I did not know any believers at that time—at least none who were close—someone with whom you can talk in the kitchen. I met the Gospel on the pages of Scripture. The Bible captured me. I read it day and night. It seemed that I read the entire Bible in just a few days. I was struck by the words of Paul: "But our citizenship is in heaven" (Phil. 3:20). This is just what I told my fellow students from the film department. I said, "You know, my home is in heaven, and I will return there someday." At that moment, they

---

10  A fermented drink prepared from mare's milk with a very low level of alcohol and an alcoholic aftertaste and smell.

thought their friend was completely crazy. Well, after reading Paul's epistles, I realized that there were at least two crazy people in the world.

But I had yet to come to church. Once again, Ruslan said, "I was invited to Kaum.[11] Please come and keep me company."

"I don't want to go anywhere." (You see, I am an introvert and hate gatherings of strangers.)

"You will have the opportunity to meet beautiful girls, and most importantly, they have no guys there."

Well, this was a persuasive argument to go to church. We came to church and saw twenty Kazakh believers in Isa Masih and, yes, half were girls. My good friend had not deceived me.

(I must say that in my opinion, girls saved more souls—at least the souls of single guys—than Billy Graham, *Superbook*, and professional preachers all put together.)

We were given a little piece of paper and began to sing songs. I'll let Ruslan describe what next transpired:

> As soon as we started singing, I felt funny. We sang, "Isa, Isa sagan uksagym keledi" (Jesus, Jesus, we want to be like You). I have a little brother named Isa. I thought, why do they want to be like him, the hooligan who always fails at school? It turns out, he is very popular here in church. Everyone wants to be like my little brother! In order not to laugh, I decided to look at my friend Kanat. In the many years of our friendship, I have never once seen him sing. And here, with sincere eyes turned upward, he sang louder than the rest.

And so, I came to church.

---

11  A Kazakh church; the literal translation from Kazakh: a gathering.

# CHAPTER 2

# DO LOCALS NEED THEIR OWN THEOLOGICAL SCHOOL?

IT WAS ALREADY ELEVEN O'CLOCK. Our small church was waiting for the meeting to begin, but our pastor was not there. Fifteen minutes later, the breathless pastor called me.

"Can you fill in for me? I have urgent business."

"What do I have to do?"

"What do you mean?! Start the meeting, preach, pray, collect the offering."

Pastor Erlan had been a believer for just four or five years. He was not a full-time minister. He earned a living as an administrator in a charitable organization and on weekends as a wedding photographer.

"Well, what do you say?"

I recalled one of my first visits to the USA. We sat in a big church, and I asked one of the brothers, "Can any of the members preach or only the pastor?"

He looked at me and said, "What are you thinking? We have professors of famous seminaries among the congregation, and even they aren't allowed to take the pulpit. Only an officially appointed pastor can preach."

But in this small church, I began to preach—without theological education, ordination, or ministry experience. This was probably the most important factor for my spiritual growth because I had to study the Scriptures more and my life had to be consistent with the sermon.

A few days later when Ruslan's parents left and we were alone in his apartment, our friend Baurzhan, deciding that sitting alone in an empty apartment is equal to a crime, immediately invited two girls over. If this had happened three months before, I would have considered it a gift from above. A few minutes later, however, I found myself driving these girls out of the apartment. After the door closed, I thought, *Who just did that?* This incident made me realize that I had changed. It certainly shocked my friends and shocked the girls even more. Their words were later passed along to me: "You tell Kanat that he is angry."

So, I got a nickname. Friends began to call me Angry.

## FAMILIARITY WITH THE SEMINARY

I was at youth camp when I first heard about the Seminary, as we called Central Asian Leadership Training Center (CALTC). Back then, I had many questions about the nature of God, the nature of man, salvation, the church, angels, etc. Our parishioners did not know the answers to these questions. One of them said, "A guy from the seminary is in camp today. He can answer your questions."

That was the first time I met a seminarian. His name was Arman, a young man of twenty, of short stature with light hair, which is unusual for a Kazakh. I approached him not with a question but with a comment. Without greeting him, I said, "I think that every person has free will and has the right to choose to follow the Lord or not. There is no destined fate that some go to Hell while others go to Heaven."

"You are a supporter of Arminius."[12]

This reply was interesting. It never occurred to me that I held the same ideas as people from Armenia. This first theological dispute ended with Arman advising me to attend CALTC the next year.

Another seminarian came up and said, "Studying there is very difficult."

Arman remarked, "It will not be difficult for him."

After this recognition of my theological talents, I could not get the thought out of my head: *Why don't I really go and study; if they could succeed, then I'll definitely succeed.*

---

12   A Dutch Protestant theologian who asserted that man is able to turn to salvation by his own free will

## TALK TO GOD

Since this was a serious decision, I decided to ask God. Several times, I'd heard students from the United States who came for the summer say that they were asking God questions. Then, we would ask them if they ever heard from God whether or not the girl they were dating was the right one. It was a terrific idea to ask God, but it turned out to be much more difficult to implement. I knelt down, read a prayer, and listened attentively; but apart from loud breathing, I did not hear anything. (When I was a teenager, my nose was broken in a karate competition, and ever since, I breathe loudly). How was I to find a way to understand the will of God? I definitely did *not* want to be like the charismatics!

Although we know that all over the world there are Presbyterians, Methodists, Pentecostals, Evangelicals, and Adventists, believers in Central Asia are divided into only two groups: Charismatics are those who speak in tongues and see visions, and everyone else is a Baptist. I proudly belonged to the second group and did not trust the methods of charismatics who had breakfast with Christ in the morning, and in the evening had dinner with the prophet Daniel. Every year, I was amused to hear about the newest book, the "latest revelation from God." The whole idea was basically that a person was taken up to Heaven where Jesus gave him the latest "word for the Church of the last days." The next year, someone else had the "latest revelation," and then the next year another, and on and on.

So, I had to find my own Baptist method for determining the will of God—and I discovered it. I thought if God speaks through Scripture, then all you need to do is to pray and open the Bible in any place, and what is written there will be the will of the Almighty. Later, I found out that this method was invented by believers long before my birth, and it's been said that thanks to this method, someone even hanged himself. In that instance, the person took a passage from Matthew, mixed it with a verse from Luke, and came to a very wrong conclusion about what God was saying.[13] But I could see no other way to know the will of God.

---

13　See Matthew 27:5b and Luke 10:37b.

I opened the Bible, and the first verse that caught my eye read, *"When they had finished eating, Jesus said to Simon Peter, 'Simon son of John, do you love me more than these?' 'Yes, Lord,' he said, 'you know that I love you.' Jesus said, 'Feed my lambs.'"*[14]

Deep down, I didn't want an answer like that. I had just graduated with honors, specializing in international economics. I wanted to work at a bank or start my own business. So, I decided to look again for a different affirmation. I closed the book, prayed again, and then re-opened it. Again, I read, *"When they had finished eating, Jesus said to Simon Peter, 'Simon son of John, do you love me more than these?' 'Yes, Lord,' he said, 'you know that I love you.' Jesus said, 'Feed my lambs.'"*

For complete conviction, I decided to close and open again.

After I read this now quite familiar dialogue for the third time, I decided that it was best for me to have dinner.

After a hearty supper, I was resolved that this method of knowing the will of God does not work because it does not give the desired result. Ah, it must be that my Bible was just bent in one place and, therefore, opened to that page all the time. I kept several copies of the Bible, which we gave to people who had just received the Lord, so I took another copy, lay down on the bed, and opened the Bible again. I discovered, to my dismay, that there is apparently nothing in the whole Bible but this one unhappy dialogue between the careless student and the patient Teacher.

And so, again I collected my things to go to the city of Almaty, which by that time had ceased to be the capital—this time for admission to the seminary.

## DIALOGUES IN DALLAS

In September of 2001, repairs were in full swing for the one-year theological school that I was hoping to attend. I stood staring at the empty eye sockets of windows and plaster falling from the ceiling like ash. One year later, in this same building, I would enroll in the Central Asian Theological Seminary (CATS). Back then, I did not know that in a few more years, as the

---

head of the development of Russian-speaking churches—which included both CALTC and CATS—I would speak out against the closure of the seminary.

But in December of 2008, I stood in our field director Bert's living room in his home on the outskirts of Dallas. In fact, Bert led everything that happened in Central Asia. We stood shouting at each other. My friend Erdos, who was head of the development of Kazakh-speaking churches, was breathing heavily and walking in circles around the sofa; he clearly did not like what was happening.

"The mission will no longer support theological education in Central Asia," said Bert.

"Why not? You promised! You said that if we put in thirty to forty thousand dollars a year, we'll keep the seminary. We found a partner seminary that will share their accreditation with us, so we will be under their covering. We recruited people and trained them for a year. When we presented the program and admitted students, we promised that they would complete a full course of study and receive a diploma."

"I did not promise them anything."

"*I* promised them."

Then I remembered that there was another seminary inside the mission, one located in Spain. "But there is an accredited seminary in Spain, fully supported by the mission. Their expenses are ten times higher than ours."

"In a year or two, that seminary will also be closed. You can bet on that."

But as far as I know, the Spanish seminary was never closed; yet many years ago, we closed our Central Asian seminary. To my knowledge, there is not a single Evangelical seminary in Kazakhstan to this day. Former teachers are now guarding shopping centers.

## ROI AND KPI IN SERVICE OF MISSION

Why did they stop supporting theological education? There are several reasons. Graduates of our seminary opened a maximum of six or seven churches each year. To our mission leaders, this was insufficient. I think the fact is that for effective management and fundraising, the mission board invited businessmen and corporate managers as executives, who then brought their business practices and corporate mentality to the mission management. One of the key tools for measuring the effectiveness of a business is Return on Investment (ROI), a financial tool which measures the gain or loss generated on an investment relative to the amount of money invested. This is used to compare the efficiency of different investments. Another tool is Key Performance Indicators (KPI), a measurable value that demonstrates how effectively a company is achieving key business objectives.

Therefore, comparing data from Central Asia and India, one can come to certain conclusions. If we and our partners established ten to twelve churches in a year, then at least a hundred appeared during the same period in India.

Such were the statistics.

But this does not show what lies behind the zeros and ones. The numbers do not show that the word "church" may conceal a group of two people or that the Gospel came to India in the twelfth century, or that *millions* of destitute people were much more willing to open their hearts to salvation. The statistics also do not say that the Gospel came to Central Asia only in the early 1990s,[15] or that all our countries are majority Muslim, or that this is one of the most difficult regions in which to spread the Kingdom of God.

Take Turkey, for example: for the last one hundred years, many missionaries have come to this country, but all these efforts have resulted in just a small number of churches with very few local believers. My wife's friend married an American and lived in Turkey. We asked if they have large churches. She replied that the churches are small, and most members are

---

15   Of course, during the times of the Soviet Union, the Orthodox church existed, but it was completely controlled by the Soviet leadership. The Union of Evangelical Christians—Baptists (ECB) was underground and could not actively preach the Gospel.

either missionaries or foreigners working in Turkey. There are very few Turkish believers.

The statistics do not say that the Kazakh central television station broadcasts programs railing against the conversion of Kazakhs to Christianity or that it is impossible to register a church. If a believer preaches the Gospel in the city in which he is not registered,[16] then this is considered to be missionary activity, and state permission is required. The numbers do not reveal that each Christian in Uzbekistan has an information card on file with the police or that if the police find a Bible in a car, they can, by law, confiscate the car. Statistics don't reveal that people are allowed to believe in Jesus but are not allowed to congregate and talk about their faith. It is impossible to enter Turkmenistan, even on a tourist visa. Once, we turned to a travel agency that promised to send us anywhere for the "right money." After six months, they told us that it's easier to find Atlantis.

All this is what the numbers cannot say.

But the numbers *will* say that the cost of living in Central Asia is rising, that renting a hall for a church meeting keeps getting more difficult and expensive,[17] that financial support for pastors has to be increased, or that a liter of gasoline is more expensive than in the USA. Looking at the numbers, one might assume that Jesus loves Hindus and Africans more because that is where he wants to spread His Kingdom, and He loves the Kazakhs, Russians, and Moldovans less.

Someone will argue that nobody determines the efficiency of Christian ministry based on ROI or KPI. I agree that these terms are not used in mission board meetings or at conferences. However, by way of example: In 2007, the main Russian television station launched the program *Stars on Ice*, where celebrities who do not figure skate perform with world champions. Former

---

16   The propiska (registration) laws require each person to be registered with the government at a physical address, and that address determines where one may be employed and receive state benefits.

17   Very few local churches own their building.

world boxing light-welterweight champion Kostya Tszyu participated in one of the shows. In 2004, he was among the best boxers on the planet pound for pound, according to *The Ring* magazine. He had fought Julio César Chávez, Zab Judah, and Ricky Hatton. In one show, Kostya performed a routine in which he lifted his partner. After the performance, the head judge, Tatiana Tarasova,[18] an outstanding coach who trained more than one generation of Olympic champions, shouted at Kostya, "Why do you always rotate your wrist? You could easily drop your partner and kill her." Kostya replied, "You know, for twenty years, I always rotated my wrist when I threw a punch. I can't do it any differently."

Therefore, a question arises regarding mission management: Is it possible to change the mindset of a person who was the division head at Walmart for forty years?

## TO THE SEMINARY AT AGE SEVENTY

Another reason my mission ceased theological training was expressed by a missionary: "Why do the Kazakhs need their own theologians? They have Timothy Keller and John Piper."

When I think about it, I remember a conversation with Ted Hutchinson, the director of our mission, about entering seminary. Back then, we young seminary teachers had a dream: to study at the Dallas Theological Seminary (DTS). There were reasons for this: Two of our best local teachers, men who greatly influenced our theological education, were graduates of this seminary. Also, DTS was famous for the course on Bible study, whose star professor was Howard Hendricks, and it was famous for in-depth study of Greek and Hebrew. DTS was for us just as Wall Street is for an investor or Pixar studio is for an animator. Very sadly, this opportunity was soon to be closed to us.

We were told that education is expensive and does not have much value in spreading the Gospel. We were given data on the growth of house

---

18   Soviet and Russian figure skating coach. Her students won forty-one gold medals at the World and European Championships, as well as eight Olympic gold medals.

churches all over the world, where it was said that many leaders who founded many home churches and cell groups did not have a theological education. Moreover, statistics showed that leaders with a similar education were less successful.

Our dreams collapsed.

Two years later, I had a conversation with Mark Gurman, a San Diego missionary working with us, who was a graduate of Moody College and father of four. He was, for many of us, like the father we never had. When you entered his office, he always looked up from his computer to smile and say how glad he was to see you. He would really listen to you, say something encouraging, and treat you to cookies or candy if he had any.

He came up to me and said, "I know you want to go to school. I was approached by Phoenix Seminary in Arizona. They told me they can sponsor one person. They will pay your full tuition; everything is free. Do you understand? Everything, including textbooks and living on campus. Go to Ted and talk to him."

Literature has many clichés—such as, "I will catch you a star," "cold as ice," "He grew wings." At that moment, I felt this last phrase in full.

Without warning the secretary, I flew into the director's office.

"Ted, I have great news! Phoenix Seminary is ready to pay for my education! Our mission won't have to pay anything. May I go and pack my bags?"

Then the unexpected happened: Ted was not happy with this news.

He said to me, "Sit down. I have already said that we are opposed to sending our people to American seminaries."

"But you said that there is no money in the budget for it, that it is too expensive. But if you had the money, you would be happy to send people to study."

Ted put his book down.

"Listen, Kanat. Now is the time to serve. After twenty or thirty years, I will personally write letters of recommendation for you to all the major seminaries. Now is not the time."

Thoughts developed and then scattered in my head. I thought, *Why would I go to seminary when I am seventy?* "Ted, you yourself studied in the seminary. You studied not only for a master's degree but also received a Ph.D. from Trinity Divinity School."

"If I could go back in time, I wouldn't study at a seminary."

And that was the end of the discussion. The seminary was ready to take me, but I wasn't allowed to go.

## IS TIMOTHY KELLER READY TO MOVE TO KAZAKHSTAN?

Returning to the statement of the missionary brother—that we don't need Kazakh theologians because we have Timothy Keller—I would not agree. First, Timothy Keller will never serve in Kazakhstan—or any other country on my side of the world. And John Piper is over seventy years old.

Second, can they find resolutions to our questions? They are not Turkic people; they do not live in a Muslim country. We have dozens, no hundreds, of unresolved theological issues which seriously affect the daily lives of believers and those who do not yet follow Jesus.

There are two diagnostic questions in Pastor D. James Kennedy's *Evangelism Explosion*—one of the most popular methods of evangelism in Evangelicalism. One question is, "Suppose that you were to die today and stand before God, and He were to say to you, 'Why should I let you into My Heaven?' What would you say?"

You know, Kazakhs are not concerned about what will happen to them after death; they worry about what their relatives say in this life. Many will not come to church, even after repenting, because they fear the condemnation of others. We tell them that they will have abundant life, but they are more concerned about how they will be buried.

For an American, a horse is a friend; for a Kazakh, it is a delicious broth and a full freezer for the winter. I heard a story of one Kazakh who moved to the USA and missed kazy-karta, a yummy horse-meat sausage, so he bought a horse and decided to slaughter it in the backyard. Needless to say, the neighbors called the police to report cruelty to animals. For Kazakhs, the most disturbing part of this story is the reaction of the neighbors.

Kazakhs, Kyrgyz, Uzbeks, and other Turkic people bake seven flatbreads every Friday, the tradition of worshiping spirits of departed ancestors. Women put the flatbread on plates, and the eldest man in the family invites all the family for prayer. Is it allowable for us to eat this bread? When a person dies in the family, the mullah gathers everyone for prayer. Can believers join and pray silently? If we do not, it will be a public insult to the whole community.

Once, a student at our seminary asked, "Is it possible to drink blood?"

"In what sense?" I replied.

"I live in the far north of Russia. And we Nenets[19] always drink reindeer blood. For us, this is a source of strength, energy, and vitamins. Vegetables and fruits are not available or are very expensive." (It's as if you paid one hundred dollars per apple in Colorado.)

This is a good question. Can we view blood as food, knowing that the Lord has cleansed everything?[20] And yet, what about Leviticus 17:14? There, we read, "Because the life of every creature is its blood. That is why I have said to the Israelites, 'You must not eat the blood of any creature, because the life of every creature is its blood; anyone who eats it must be cut off.'" I doubt that even experienced theologians will come to a common opinion in this matter.

And how about this story: A recent Afghan convert was taught that a true Christian should have but one wife. So, he comes home, keeps one wife (I assume the youngest), and the other wives are told to return to their parents with their children; from now on, he will have just one wife. After that, one of the abandoned wives drenches herself with gasoline and sets herself on

---

19  A people group inhabiting the extreme north of Russia
20  See Peter's vision in Acts 10.

fire. (I do not know if this story is true, for not all missionary stories can be trusted). However, since I, too, am from a Stan country, I think it is quite plausible. It is a terrible shame for a married woman in a Muslim country to return to her parents. Also, women do not work. Losing a husband means losing one's food. Who will now care for the children of this Christian?

Will Alistair McGrath, R.C. Sproul, John MacArthur, Gordon Fee, or Charles Ryrie be able to answer these questions?

If there are no Kazakh, Chinese, or Arab theologians, then you shouldn't have teachers either because no teacher creates his training course from scratch. If a professor teaches a course in marketing, he does not create the concept of marketing, does not invent the philosophy of marketing, and does not invent the methods of marketing. In addition to his experience, he borrows theoretical content from Theodor Levitt, Philip Kotler, and Jack Trout. If he teaches mathematics, he turns to Sir Isaac Newton or Gregory Perelman. If he teaches acting skills, he follows Konstantin Stanislavsky, Sanford Meisner, and Uta Hagen.

And to whom should a local pastor or teacher come when preparing for a sermon, Bible study group, or conference? Of course, he can read John Calvin, Leon Morris, or Wayne Grudem, but do they have the answers to our questions? I am speaking about cultural and regional issues like the ones above. If a marketing professor in an MBA program cannot answer the questions of his students, what is the danger? The students will get less knowledge? They may lose sales? They may not be able to develop a successful marketing strategy based on the competitive environment? The danger is much higher for lack of a healthy theology.

Leave aside cultural and regional issues, and let's talk about theology in general. Timothy Keller is far away, and the pastor is near. If a pastor does not need to study, if it's enough for him just to repent and have a Bible, he may come to the same conclusion as one pastor in the Ukraine: if a husband and wife do not have a unified vision regarding the ministry, then  he will conduct a special course called, "How to Properly Divorce and Bring Double Glory to the Lord." Another pastor, leading the largest Kazakh ministry of five hundred people, teaches that believers no longer need to repent of their sins because, according to the Scriptures, we are gods. And can a god repent before God?

What about corruption? Several times a year we, as parents of a schoolgirl, must give money for different items, including a fee for a "committee meeting," a state committee that inspects the school regarding grades, discipline, etc. In reality, this is one form of a bribe; the money pays committee members to give a favorable review. And this "tradition" exists in all cities, in all schools, throughout the country.

Should we pay these "fees"? I do. If I don't, the teacher may be fired, or the teacher, who like all teachers receives the lowest salary in the country, will have to pay that fee out of pocket in order to preserve his job.

In the first year of my conversion, I worked as a sales representative at a food company. Officers of the financial police (like the IRS in the USA) came to our director and demanded their "share." He refused to pay. The next day, they impounded all the trucks of the company. The director filed a lawsuit, and the company suffered losses as the suit proceeded. We won the trial and had our trucks returned, but all the food had been smashed against the walls of the trucks. The next day when the trucks left on their routes, they were again impounded. We won the trial again. And the trucks were again impounded. In the end, the company had to pay. In his place, what would I do?

Some say, "If that's the situation, then don't do business." That can't be the answer. If it is, then in any post-Soviet country, a Christian cannot be a businessman, policeman, taxman, architect, teacher, civil servant, lawyer, restaurateur, engineer, judge, security guard, minister, doctor, or director. Whatever you do, one way or another, you come across bribes, kickbacks, and theft. And it's not about individual people; it's about the system itself. Are we just to quit working, go home, hide in a corner, and cover ourselves with a blanket and die?

A friend of mine said, "I didn't want to live in sin, so I moved to Canada." In my opinion, that's not the best theological decision.

## JONATHAN EDWARDS OF CENTRAL ASIA

If you look at the history of the church, it's clear that without strong theological training, there is no strong church. This training can come from individuals, a school, or a movement, such as the following:

- At the time of the apostles, they had Paul, John, and Peter.
- The post-apostolic period before the Council of Nicaea had Clement of Rome, Ignatius of Antioch, Tertullian, and Origen.
- Before the fall of the Roman Empire, there were Athanasius of Alexandria, the Cappadocian fathers, John Chrysostom, Jerome, and Augustine.
- During the time of the medieval church and scholasticism, there were Anselm of Canterbury, Thomas Aquinas, and John Wycliffe.
- The Reformation showcased Martin Luther, John Calvin, Ulrich Zwingli, and John Knox.
- The Age of Enlightenment was the time of Jonathan Edwards, George Whitefield, and John Wesley.
- Modern times included Charles Spurgeon, Dwight Moody, Benjamin Warfield, and Charles Hodge.
- Even in the darkest time of the twentieth century, during the flowering of fascism, Dietrich Bonhoeffer and Karl Barth were leading the way in Germany.

Let's say that a gifted theologian leaves his post as head of the Old Testament Department at Trinity Seminary in Chicago and decides to settle in the north of Kazakhstan. He must learn the Kazakh language, become familiar with the culture, and start attending a local church. Certainly, he will try to answer our questions. However, he needs to understand that his theology will not be only biblical, it will also be American. Surely, he will bring his Chicago to Kazakhstan, completely unaware that he is doing so. As one of the professors at our closed seminary said, "Each of us wears glasses that he doesn't suspect: cultural glasses, denominational glasses, his-own-experience glasses."

Do Kazakhs need theologians?

If we say no, then we also do not need teachers, preachers, pastors, evangelists—even the Church is not needed. And here we come to the only correct logical conclusion: then Kazakhs do not need Jesus either.

CHAPTER 3

# EXPERIMENTS ON A LIVING BODY

AN ASSISTANT COMES TO THE pastor and says, "What are we going to do, Pastor? People are leaving the church!"

"I have an idea. Let's make a cell church. The church will grow threefold. Guaranteed."

"Great, Pastor!"

A month later, the assistant comes again and asks, "What shall we do, Pastor? People are still leaving the church! Half the church is already gone!"

"I have a new idea. Let's join the movement of house churches. We won't need a building, and everything is informal."

"Great, Pastor!"

A month later, the assistant says, "What are we going to do, Pastor? People keep leaving! Only the leaders are left!"

"I know exactly what to do. The latest word in the Christian world is the organic church. This alone is the true biblical design."

"Great, Pastor!"

A month later, here comes the assistant again. "Pastor, the organic church didn't work. Only I am left."

"That's too bad because I still have many more good ideas . . ."

—Anecdote from Central Asia

\*\*\*

On the phone, we continued to argue. My boss didn't understand why I had not conducted the *4 Fields of Jesus' Strategy*, a program for multiplying healthy disciples and churches,[21] at churches in my region. He also wondered if I had found good partners. The rest of my colleagues had not only found partners but also had actively taught the theories. But I wanted to try things for myself, to see the result and only then offer it to others, and I didn't care if it took several years.

"But we don't have that much time," came the answer.

I did not give up. "Remember how many different strategies we implemented and what came out of them." The person on the other end of the line was ready to hang up, but I knew that he would not.

For many years, the focus of our mission was to train future leaders. Therefore, in partnership with local churches where our graduates held leadership positions, we started schools that taught many courses, including Bible Study Methods, Old and New Testaments, Systematic Theology, Pastoral Theology, and Leadership. For outreach, we partnered with key churches that were open to collaboration. Some were Baptist, Presbyterian, or Pentecostal, but most of the churches were non-denominational; they simply called themselves Evangelical. Our partners were located throughout Central Asia.

At one point, the mission leadership changed its focus from training leaders to church planting. Now we were required to start churches, quickly and in large quantities. In order to achieve this goal, we came to our partners, and it was on them that we tested the newest methods of church multiplication. Our partner churches were traditional, and not all pastors agreed with our proposed strategies. Some left; most remained. It was among them that a new breed appeared: Frankenstein churches.

On these churches, we used all the methods known to the modern Evangelical church: cell, home, G-12, organic, powerful Chinese "3" cells. Of course, there is nothing wrong with various forms of church meetings, but the paradox was that in our case, they were the same churches. We tried a method;

21   "Resources for Multiplying Healthy Disciples and Churches," e3Partners.org, https://e3partners.org/training/ (accessed October 11, 2020).

and if it did not work, then we implemented another. That is why I call them Frankenstein churches. Victor Frankenstein created a being from fragments of dead bodies and then tried to find a way to revive him. We did the same.

Like Frankenstein, the result horrified me. Churches were dying and splitting. Those who managed to survive were like ghosts. Like Victor Frankenstein, who dreamed of giving people hope, to make the lame walk, and to change the world, we dreamed of creating churches that would grow and multiply, quickly. This is what we wanted to see and the direction we were going.

But our teachers, as I later understood, had one major misconception. They believed that the single most important aspect of church growth is an effective church model, a model which has been proven to work. You know, this is akin to a magic formula. If you find the right magic formula it will work anywhere, anytime, with anyone. Automatically.

Every year, they came to us, or we ourselves went to conferences where we met people who had spent years leading home or cell churches in India, Indonesia, or China. The founders came in person or sent their representatives. We were amazed and bewitched by the powerful movement of the Holy Spirit in these countries. They told us of a region in India that ten years ago did not have a single meeting and now has more than ten thousand. I don't remember the numbers, but I remember that they were huge. At the conferences, we loudly applauded and glorified God for the amazing work that He has done in these countries. This data captured our minds and motivated us to do something similar here in Central Asia. At these conferences, we were practically guaranteed that if we use these methods, then the results would exceed all our expectations.

Well, it turned out that these methods absolutely refused to work in Central Asia.

I was also embarrassed that the methods we taught to church leaders were not tested by ourselves; we believed in these methods because we were told to believe in them. But they did not work. People did not want to repent. Church members were not impressed. Leaders were on fire and then burned out.

Over time, my doubts grew. Therefore, at the next seminar, I approached the speaker and asked questions: How many house churches did you personally open? In which country? In what city? How many people attended each meeting? Do leaders get support from the mission?

Well, the teachers were not at all pleased with the questions. They gave vague answers. It often turned out that they had attended this seminar in somewhere like Thailand, and one of their homework assignments was to pass this information on to others. But, they added, even if they themselves had not opened a single church, this doesn't mean that these methods don't work.

I had even more doubts after Brother Ivan's trip to India. We were told so much about the strikingly large movement of house churches in our Indian division that it was decided to send someone from Central Asia to exchange experiences. According to the data, at that time, our mission had more than six hundred home churches in India. Ivan was inspired by the upcoming trip and wanted to personally see the wondrous works of God.

Two weeks later, upon his return, I had prepared a list of questions all with a basic meaning: How do they do it?

It turned out that Ivan got three things out of the trip:

1.   He attended a seminar at the mission headquarters for a week.
2.   He and a local believer did street evangelism using the CAMEL method. Camel is an acronym for Chosen Angels Miracles Eternal Life. This method of evangelism aims to win Muslims to Christ by using passages about Jesus found in the Quran.
3.   He liked the Taj Mahal very much.

I asked, "Did you see a huge movement of churches in different regions among different nationalities?"

He answered, "Well, I visited one group."

"What about others? In two weeks, you could have visited at least ten home churches."

He said that the director of the Indian mission had forbidden it because the presence of a foreigner would have a negative impact on the community. This was hard to understand. When a few years earlier we went on a similar trip to Urumqi in western China, I could understand why we were not allowed to attend a single group. In China, people go to prison for their faith. But I could not understand why it would be so in India, a country of Hindus, where the state tolerates the preaching of the Gospel—even if there can be strong persecution from family and neighbors.

Of course, I am not saying that everything we were told about the work in India, China, or Indonesia is not true. I do not live there and have not served there. I cannot speak for those countries, but I can speak for Central Asia.

In the introduction of David Garrison's book *Church Planting Movements* (the bible of home church proponents) under the heading "Central Asia," we read, "A strategy coordinator reports: Around the end of 1996, we called around to the various churches in the area and got their count on how many had come to faith in that one year. When they were all added up, it came to 15,000 baptisms in one year. The previous year we estimated only 200 believers altogether."[22]

In my ten years of full-time ministry, I have met many key leaders from Kazakhstan, Uzbekistan, Kyrgyzstan, Tajikistan, and even inaccessible Turkmenistan. Some were believers during the Soviet times—Russian Baptists and Pentecostals. They have no idea where these figures come from.

Someday, I may happen to meet Mr. Garrison, and I would like to know the name of this mysterious strategy coordinator and in which Central Asian country he lives. With what mission does he work? And most importantly, where did he get this data?

---

22  David Garrison, *Church Planting Movements: How God is Redeeming a Lost World* (Monument: WIGTake Resources LLC, 2004).

## BUILDING ON SOMEONE ELSE'S FOUNDATION

Such reflections had led me to the telephone conversation with my boss that started this chapter. I no longer wanted to teach these church development methods. I only wanted to teach those things with which I had direct experience and had seen a positive result.

I thought, *Why can't we build churches from scratch? Why must we work with existing churches?* I pondered the words of Paul: "It has always been my ambition to preach the gospel where Christ was not known, so that I would not be building on someone else's foundation. Rather, as it is written: 'Those who were not told about him will see, and those who have not heard will understand.'"[23] Paul purposefully went to people who had not yet heard the Gospel. Why aren't we doing this?

Mission leaders have graduated from respected seminaries: Gordon Conwell, Moody, Southwestern Baptist Theological Seminary, Dallas Theological Seminary, Fuller Theological Seminary. The study of Paul's Epistles is a core curriculum of Evangelical seminaries. There are more than one hundred commentaries on the Epistle to the Romans, including those written by Hodge, Murray, Moo, MacArthur, and Morris.

Douglas Moo writes, "Paul here indicates that he believed that God had given him the ministry of establishing strategic churches in virgin gospel territory; like the early American pioneers who pulled up stakes any time they could see the smoke from another person's cabin, Paul felt 'crowded' by too many Christians."[24]

Why don't missions follow Paul's advice? Of course, I don't mean all missions. I know at least one mission that tries to start churches from scratch. And I don't mean the place that Douglas Moo is talking about—virgin Gospel territory. Even though there are some churches in Central Asia, it remains one of the most unreached regions. The number of believers does not exceed

---

23   Romans 15:20-21
24   Douglas.J. Moo, *The Epistle to the Romans* (Grand Rapids: Wm. B. Eerdmans Publishing Co., 1996) p. 896.

0.1 percent, even by the most positive estimates. When I say that we should not build on someone else's foundation, I mean the local church.

## FAST FOOD CHRISTIANITY

So, why don't missions start their own churches—or at least help local ministers start meetings from the ground up—in order to try out their "unique" methods? Why should they come to existing churches?

There are reasons for this. One reason is the desire to get quick results. Ray Kroc's system has done its job. Kroc was the long-time chairman of McDonald's, the world's most famous fast food chain. Today's world worships speed. Brian Edler, owner of four Domino's Pizza franchises in Ohio, made history in 2010, entering *The Guinness Book of Records* by producing 204 pizzas in an hour. Shinkansen, a network of high-speed bullet trains with a maximum speed of 360 miles per hour, covers the distance between Osaka and Tokyo (277 miles)in two hours and twenty-five minutes, including stops in Yokohama, Nagoya, and Kyoto. In the USA, my friend told me why he decided to leave a high-tech company where he earned good money. He said, "For example, I create a program and work on it around the clock. I don't sleep; I don't see my family; and after six months, it's out of date."

The era of fast food gave birth to Fast Food Christianity. If a mission asks its ministers to start meetings from scratch, in Central Asia, it will take from four to six years to build a congregation of forty people, and there are no guarantees even for that. For each successful church, there are ten meetings that never really get off the ground or disappear over time.

Therefore, our mission needed magic formulas to multiply existing churches. But as you understand from what I've written above, nothing happened. After several experiments, observations, and reflections, I stopped believing in the existence of a "magic formula."

I will give one observation that supports my conclusions: Once, a team of evangelists came to us from our central office in Dallas. This team was led by Bryan Johnson, the pastor of a large church in Texas. He and his wife conducted a course on Christian marriage in our seminary. He had a wonderful family. He began each course with an impressive introduction:

"Hello, my name is Bryan. I have been married for forty years. I have three children and six grandchildren, and I've been in the ministry for forty years."

When we preach the Gospel, we often say that by accepting Jesus Christ as your Lord and Savior, you will have eternal life and joy in this life. I do not know whether all believers personify the example of a joyful life, but Bryan did. When remembering a person, it's interesting that most often you remember their face: someone thoughtful, dissatisfied, joyful. When I remember Bryan, I always remember him smiling.

Once, Bryan brought a team of evangelists. We met with the team, and they shared their plans. They had just come from Cuba, and God was doing amazing things there. They had knocked on doors, and everyone they talked to was touched by the Gospel in a special way. According to them, every second person accepted Jesus as their Lord, some kneeling and in tears. It seemed they brought Cuba with them. Their faces shone, and their hearts danced to "Guantanamera." They said, "You will see what amazing things God will do here in Kazakhstan."

Then they gave us advice and recommendations on how to properly turn people to God. After class, they went out to preach the Gospel, while we stayed behind to prepare for our lectures and check homework.

Every evening, they returned to the mission building; and every evening, their faces grew gloomier. They stopped coaching us. On their final day, it seemed they wanted to depart unnoticed.

My friend Ruslan worked in our mission as a translator. He went to see them off. Bryan said, "Ruslan, I want to give you my jacket. I don't need it, but you may need it." He gave Ruslan his jacket and merrily walked to the plane wearing just a T-shirt, and a smile still shone on his face. It was cold outside—ten degrees Celsius (fifty degrees Fahrenheit).

I later learned from the brothers who accompanied the team that not one single person repented in all those days of street evangelism.

Here I would like to stop and work it out. Why?

Let's take a look: here were the same preachers, the same Gospel, the same methods, the same God. In Cuba, every other person repents; in Kazakhstan, not even one.

This is why I do not believe what I was told. I no longer believe promises like, "Do the G-12 method, and you will get the same results." Cesar Castellanos' ministry in Bogota, Colombia, currently has twenty-five thousand members. We can say that this strategy works just fine in Bogota, but let's look at the church in Senim, Kazakhstan,[25] which has used this same strategy for ten years in Central Asia. Today, this assembly has just 150 people.

The Yoido Full Gospel Church, a Pentecostal church in South Korea founded by Pastor David Yonggi Cho, is the largest Christian parish in the world. It united more than a million members in 587 churches. The home church in Seoul is attended by 830,000 members. The Almaty branch of the Yoido church has about seventy-five people.

Consider Vineyard churches. This dynamic worldwide movement, started by John Wimber, did much to help the church believe that God can speak directly to people as well as heal and work miracles. In Kazakhstan, there are forty members.[26]

Over the last ten years, the growth of the Church in Central Asia has basically ceased, though we see just a few growing churches that have added several people. Most pastors and leaders fear losing what they have.

Also, I don't want to say that Cesar Castellanos's G-12, Yonggi Cho's cell church, or Neil Cole's organic church do not work. I believe that models may be more or less suitable based on the culture, mentality, and financial resources of a particular region.

---

25  The name has been changed.
26  I'm not sure if this church was an official branch of Vineyard; but the pastor was a member of Vineyard in the USA, and he called his church a Vineyard church.

After all, it is easier for villagers to gather for a cup of tea at home than in the conference hall of a hotel. Older Europeans would prefer to gather in a church building than on the grass in a nearby park. Muslims will not enter a building with a large cross on the facade.

## WHO IS THE FAIREST OF THEM ALL?

I do not want to criticize this or that model, though I used to do this all the time. Perhaps this was partly due to the fact that each new model consciously or unconsciously criticized what came before it. Of course, you will rarely find direct criticism in the books, but in one way or another, it is inferred at seminars, conferences, and in private conversations.

For example, the cell church criticized the traditional church. The tremendous amount of money they spend on buildings could be spent on evangelism or helping the poor. They must pay many ministers, but cell group leaders are unpaid lay people who could be architects, sales agents, or teachers. The preachers are mostly professional pastors, but in a cell, any believer can preach. The church is not a building but a collection of followers of Jesus.

The apologists of home churches condemned the pursuit of growth by the leaders of the cell church. Cells were divided not because the necessary growth cycle had occurred, but because it was necessary to achieve the goal for the year. Cell churches began to resemble a corporation. For just as a company sets a goal to earn one hundred million dollars a year, the cell church sets the goal for one hundred cells a year. The achievement of this goal became a higher priority than the action of the Holy Spirit. For the sake of rapid growth and achievement of the annual leadership goal, people who were not prepared or spiritually mature were put in leadership. One cell leader taught that the Trinity is not entirely clear and is an outdated concept; another taught *Rich Dad, Poor Dad* by Robert Kiyosaki and Sharon Lechter, instead of the Bible; and a third was flirting with sisters.

Supporters of the organic church said that home churches are just traditional churches gathering in houses. Over time, they turn into closed clubs for the elite and are strictly by invitation. There is no clear understanding of church planting. Tithes are not collected as the church ceases to need funding; and if tithes are not collected, then believers stop trusting God—at least, for their material needs.

Comparisons arise naturally. When one says something is better, bigger, more beautiful, we at least internally ask the question, "Compared with what?" If we say that Toyota is a quality car, then we ask, "Compared to what other brand—Hyundai, Chevrolet, or Skoda?" If Toyota were the only car company in the world, how would we know it was a quality car?

In the same way, the advantages of a new church development plan were often negatively compared with what went before.

My mentor, Mark, taught our Church Planting course every year. In the class, we studied *Church Dynamics* by Gene Getz, *Missionary Methods* by Roland Allen, *Natural Church Development* by Christian Schwarz. But most of all, I remember one phrase from Rick Warren's book *The Purpose Driven Church:* "Never criticize what God is blessing."[27]

Concluding this chapter, I want to say:

There is no magic formula.

There is no magic formula.

There is no magic formula.

There is no magic formula.

There is no magic formula.

There is no magic formula.

That said, I am quite sure that church development fads will persist—the latest church planting theories, new training techniques, secret methods of evangelism. Sadly, people have always had, and will always have, a craving for

---

27   Rick Warren, *The Purpose Driven Church: Every Church is Big in God's Eyes* (Grand Rapids: Zondervan, 1995).

magic formulas promising quick results, like how to become a millionaire in a month or learn a foreign language in two days.

# CHAPTER 4

# SO, WHAT IS THE POINT?

*The LORD said, "Go out and stand on the mountain in the presence of the LORD, for the LORD is about to pass by." Then a great and powerful wind tore the mountains apart and shattered the rocks before the LORD, but the LORD was not in the wind. After the wind there was an earthquake, but the LORD was not in the earthquake. After the earthquake came a fire, but the LORD was not in the fire. And after the fire came a gentle whisper.*[28]

I WILL NOT RETELL HERE what happened to Elijah on Mount Horeb, for the story is well known. Yet, these words astound me.

Imagine you are going to New York, and your friend asks you to deliver a package to a person. He gives you these instructions: "By nine o'clock, you will reach Christopher Street and 6th Avenue. Initially, you will pass by a huge man, like a basketball player, wearing a Miami Heat shirt. It's not him. Then, an elderly man with gray hair will drive up in a BMW 5 model. He will get out his car and enter a shop. This is not him either. You'll see a grandmother sitting on a bench feeding pigeons. It is definitely not her. Then, a ten-year-old girl with a white backpack will step off a bus. This is the one. Give her the package."

This is a strange set of instructions. Couldn't you just say a ten-year-old girl with a white backpack will step off the bus? Not in this case. God wants to teach us something along with Elijah.

---

28   1 Kings 19:11-12

Tremendously large trucks work at coal mines—Terex from Canada, Caterpillar from the USA, Komatsu from Japan—but the biggest mining truck of all was produced in Belarus, the Belaz 75710: sixty-nine feet long, twenty-six feet high, weighing 360 tons. No one would attach tricycle wheels to such a huge truck; they don't do justice to the size. Similarly, we humans think that if God is great, then we must characterize Him with something great.

Look carefully at the passage. A wind destroying mountains is nothing more than a hurricane. Every adult has an idea of an earthquake. Even children know about forest fires. These are things you cannot ignore.

A hurricane blowing cows around and draining rivers attracts attention. What about the California wildfires in December of 2017, which were compared to Mordor? We live in Almaty, a seismically active zone with the possibility of an earthquake of eight or higher on the Richter scale. You don't ignore those; even a little shaking is enough to make me stare at the ceiling all night and watch the chandelier closely.

Yet, who pays attention to the whispering wind? It's ordinary, happens every day. Who would upload a video with the title, "Shocking! Must Watch! We had a light breeze in Portland today!"

We are passionate about our hurricanes, fires, and earthquakes and never pay attention to the gentle breeze.

## WHY DON'T BELIEVERS PREACH THE GOSPEL?

A study conducted by LifeWay Research concluded that that eighty-five percent of all believers ages eighteen to twenty-nine say they should share the Gospel with unbelievers, though only twenty-five percent of them look for ways to do so.[29]

Researcher Ed Stetzer gives four reasons why people do not preach the Gospel:

---

29   Ed Stetzer, "The State of Evangelism," Christianity Today.com, May 12, 2014, https://www.christianitytoday.com/edstetzer/2014/may/state-of-evangelism.html.

- "I'm afraid they'll ask questions I can't answer."
- "I struggle with my own faith."
- "I never learned how."
- "I don't know how to start a conversation."[30]

In Kazakhstan, we receive similar answers. (Perhaps another answer is that people don't have enough time.) Since most of the answers concerned ignorance or inability, we trained people to preach the Gospel using *The Four Spiritual Laws* and other guidebooks explaining the first steps in discipleship.

However, after teaching many people the four spiritual laws, we did not see an increase in evangelism. Upon reflection, we came to the conclusion that this method is too simple and does not explain in detail the sinfulness of man, the need for repentance, the righteousness of God, and the cross of Christ. We thought this was the reason we failed.

We found a method that not only explained the key points of the Christian faith but also included apologetic evidence, multiple Scriptures, and questions that made people think about their lives. However, the most important factor was emphasis on practical experience. The Evangelism Explosion taught people not only the importance of evangelism but also how to actually do it. The four spiritual laws also had a practical aspect, but I never saw such a well-thought-out system as Evangelism Explosion. Everything was planned: who is going where, who is accompanying them, and what the purpose is of each particular outreach.

First, the teacher witnesses and shows by personal example how this is done. Then, the student follows the teacher's example. Following that, there is a time of analysis: what happened, what did not work out, what can be done better, what to do next time, etc. If necessary, the mentor again takes the reins and shows the correct way. The student carefully observes the element with which he struggled, which could be giving a testimony, asking intentional questions, or making a call for repentance.

30  Jesus Film Project, "4 Reasons People Give for Not Sharing the Gospel," JesusFilm.org, October 26, 2017, https://www.jesusfilm.org/blog-and-stories/4-reason-not-sharing.html.

We expected a real explosion after the introduction of this method, but it was more like a Chinese firecracker—it just made a lot of noise. Then, just like on the first day of the new year when you find scattered, ragged remnants of firecrackers and bottle rockets, you find pieces of workbooks under your bed, and they are not even from last year.

Even after learning how to start a conversation and answer difficult questions, church members did not race to preach the Gospel. It's no secret that this also applies to us mentors, pastors, seminary teachers, and media ministers. Seminary teachers especially like to justify themselves, making excuses with teachings about gifts. They say, "I'd rather be a good teacher than a bad evangelist."

## CAN YOU BELIEVE EVERYTHING YOU HEAR?

What is wrong here? It seems that you can't believe everything people say. Consider this marketing paradox: Company A decides to market a specific product and polls thousands of respondents from the target audience: Are you willing to buy this product? Does the price suit you? What problems can it solve for you? Having received a positive reaction, the company decides to launch the product, only to find that the very people who said they wanted to buy it will not actually buy it.

When I started a training company (in later chapters I will return to this period of my life), I met with many HR directors and offered to conduct trainings. I often received this common response: "We would really like to use your services, but we don't have funds budgeted at the moment." The most annoying thing was to find out a week later that they bought training from another company.

People are unwilling, sometimes without even realizing it, to give honest answers for various reasons. They cannot simply say, "You are a new company, and we doubt that you can give us the result we expect," or "Your training topic does not suit us." Therefore, sales experts advise one to ask why several times when meeting with customers. Perhaps the client will speak truthfully after the fifth time.

So, out of the four answers received by Ed Stetzer, the true objection, I think, is, "I struggle with my own faith." I would not take the other three into account.

Going beyond the earthquakes, we finally arrive at the quiet wind. But can we recognize it?

## A PEASANT WITHOUT A NAME

In the film *The Seven Samurai*, peasants from a small village decide to hire samurai to defend them against robbers. To this end, they go to the city where they find the first samurai, who explains to the peasants that two or three samurai will not be enough to protect the village; seven are needed. To hire experienced samurai, they come up with various tests for candidates. Some agree to the job, and some leave offended, for the peasants could not pay money and offered only shelter and food. When the group of hired samurai is ready to leave the city, a nameless peasant tries to join them. All he has to prove himself is a stolen Samurai family pedigree. By it, he tries to prove that he is one of them. But he was not a skilled swordsman, nor did he have any years of service to a lord, nor had he led troops into battle. He pretended to be someone that he was not.[31]

How can we talk about what we don't know or draw what we have not seen? Can we be a witness if we haven't witnessed anything?

Leo Tolstoy said "A person who has nothing to say usually speaks a lot." As ministers, we do talk about God a lot, but do we have something to say?

Certainly, we can remember slogans:

- "The only way to God is through Christ."
- "We will be resurrected on the last day."
- "Seek first his kingdom and his righteousness."[32]

---

31  Akira Kurosawa, director, *Seven Samurai*, Toho Company, 1956.
32  Matthew 6:33

- "For God so loved the world that he gave his one and only Son, that whoever believes in him shall not perish but have eternal life."[33]

One may also remember the Chalcedon Creed. This is all good.

However, is this not similar to the stolen pedigree of the nameless peasant? The pedigree is valid but is not our own. I do not want to say that many Christians are not believers. (And yes, some people who call themselves Christians are not believers.) I do want to say that there are married couples who do not know each other. Bryan Johnson, the same pastor who led the evangelism team and taught us about marriage, called this a "union of married singles." So are we with God. We have entered into a union with God, but do we know Him?

*Seven Samurai* was directed by Akira Kurosawa, considered one of the outstanding filmmakers in the history of cinema, along with Federico Fellini, Antonioni, Alfred Hitchcock, and Tarkovsky. Once a journalist asked Kurosawa, "What does the cinema mean to you?" He replied, "It is simple: take myself, subtract movies, and the result is zero."[34] Can we reply in a similar way? Can we say, "If you take God away from me, then the result is zero"? Or will many things remain?

Luke Freeman taught the doctrine of the Church at our seminary. We once asked him, "What are your priorities in life? What is first for you; what is second; what is third?" We were interested to know—and of course, we understood—that there is no definite answer. For example, American missionaries put God first and family second. Korean missionaries put God first and ministry second. He replied, "I don't put anything in first, second, or third place. I look at my schedule and see what took my time last week. This is how I understand my priorities."

This is correct. We may say that our family occupies an important place in our lives; but if we don't spend time with our children, if we don't go on

---

33   John 3:16
34   Shawn Swanky, *How to Improve Your Movie Literacy with Akira Kurosawa* (Morrisville: Lulu.com, 2016).

date nights with our spouse, and if the last time we had a family vacation was seven years ago, then it is all just words.

My friend Konstantin is the pastor of a large cell church in Uzbekistan. During its heyday, it had more than one hundred cells. Once, I asked him, "How do you choose cell leaders?"

"I don't choose them. The state does it for me."

"How so?"

"As soon as a new member joins our group, they are called in for questioning by the security department.[35] After that, some continue to believe, and some publicly burn their Bibles. Something like this."

Two weeks ago, as I was preparing to preach on a passage in Matthew chapter nine, I thought how interesting it is that we pastors urge our members to evangelize, yet they do not. But Jesus, on the contrary, forbade some to talk about Himself, yet they still told others.

*"Jesus warned them sternly, 'See that no one knows about this.' But they went out and spread the news about him all over that region."*[36]

Why did they not listen to Jesus? Why didn't they keep quiet? Why did they not hide under their beds? Something had happened to them, something so great that they could not hide it. They wanted to share what they had experienced with the world.

Each and every one of us has met God. What made us forget the whispering wind?

---

35  SNB (Service of National Security), a post-Soviet analogue of the KGB; equivalent to the FBI in the USA
36  Matthew 9:30-31

# CHAPTER 5
# LOSS OF THE WHISPERING WIND

I LOOKED AT THE CLOCK. 6:45 p.m. I wondered, should I go for pizza or wait for the guests? Unpeeled carrots sat next to the skillet. I put all this in the pantry. Another fight, and once again my wife, Dinara, left the house right before the home group began. When people arrived, I knew what to say: "Mother called Dinara. Something happened again, so Dinara had to leave." I knew this was a lie, but don't I have to conform to the ideal image of a minister?!

Six months later, we held a meeting in the house of Sister Zhana. I came half an hour early. In the bedroom, Brother Dauren was changing the baby as I stood with him. The front door creaked open. Zhana walked into the kitchen and yelled, "Why haven't you washed the dishes, you morons?" (The morons were her husband and younger brother.) Dauren replied, "Kanat is here." Zhana said from the kitchen, "Why didn't you warn me?"

I like to watch the brothers and sisters when they think that no one sees them. For example, in a mall, they look like normal people—sometimes strict, sometimes careless, sometimes happy, sometimes sad. These are mementos of my service in the church.

In the afternoon, I taught at seminary; in the evening and on weekends, I was one of the church leaders. In the afternoon, I taught theory; in the evening, I watched how theory was put into practice. Watching this process, I wondered if, like a house, we needed to have a front door and a back door.

I noticed that there is an extraordinary power in the piece of wood called the threshold of a church. No matter how hard people are fighting and arguing right in front of the church, as soon as their foot crosses that piece of wood, everything changes. Smiles appear; mouths fill with compliments. My family was no exception.

Our church was like a theater. The theater is based on dramatic action, primarily expressed by an actor. Uta Hagen—an acting teacher whose students included Robert De Niro, Whoopi Goldberg, and Jack Lemmon—said that acting is more difficult than playing a musical instrument or dancing.[37] She is quite right. The pianist and the piano are separate from each other. The actor is both artist and canvas. The actor must pretend to be joyful, even after he wrecked his car on the way to the theater. We, also, like professional actors, strive to portray fun, happiness, and delight.

We are told:

- "You are the light of the world."[38]
- "I will say it again: Rejoice!"[39]
- "I have come that [you] may have life . . . to the full."[40]

We put on a show in order to conform with the Scriptures. First of all, we play pretend in front of non-believers so as not to cause them to stumble over the Gospel, and then we play-act before each other. The trouble is, Christians are very bad actors.

I like Oscar Wilde's story, *The Star-Child*. Two woodcutters are walking through the forest and notice a falling star. Hoping to find gold where it fell, they instead find a child wrapped in a golden cloak. One of them takes the boy and raises him among his own children. The boy grows to be beautiful in appearance but ugly on the inside. He despises the villagers

---

37  Jamie Marsh, "Uta Hagen's Acting Class part 1,"October 5, 2015, YouTube video, 1:32:14, https://www.youtube.com/watch?v=SseJhOPV9nY.

38  Matthew 5:14

39  Philippians 4:4

40  John 10:10

and hates his brothers. He throws stones at the blind and the poor. Once, he sees a beggar woman under a tree. "See! There sitteth a foul beggar-woman under that fair and green-leaved tree. Come, let us drive her hence, for she is ugly and ill-favoured." Later he discovers that the beggar is his own mother.[41]

Doesn't that seem like us? In appearance, we are beautiful. We dress decently, say beautiful words, do the right things. But inside of us, something is wrong. Just as the star boy did not recognize his mother, we do not perceive the whispering wind.

## DO WE STILL NEED THE BOOK OF PSALMS?

In the seminary, one of the courses I taught was "Bible Study Methods: Genre Poetry." This genre includes Psalms, Proverbs, Ecclesiastes, Song of Songs, and Job. I pondered verses from the Psalms:

In the morning, LORD, you hear my voice;
in the morning I lay my requests before you
and wait expectantly.[42]

Hear my voice when I call, LORD;
be merciful to me and answer me.
My heart says of you, "Seek his face!"
Your face, LORD, I will seek.
Do not hide your face from me,
do not turn your servant away in anger;
you have been my helper.
Do not reject me or forsake me,
God my Savior.

41   Oscar Wilde, *The Star-Child* (Edinburgh: Floris Books, 1999).
42   Psalm 5:3

Though my father and mother forsake me,
the LORD will receive me.[43]

As the deer pants for streams of water,
so my soul pants for you, my God.
My soul thirsts for God, for the living God.
When can I go and meet with God?[44]

You, God, are my God,
earnestly I seek you;
I thirst for you,
my whole being longs for you,
in a dry and parched land
where there is no water.
I have seen you in the sanctuary
and beheld your power and your glory.[45]

I also compared those verses with these from the book of Hosea:

Hear the word of the LORD, you Israelites,
because the LORD has a charge to bring
against you who live in the land:
"There is no faithfulness, no love,
no acknowledgment of God in the land."[46]

"Let us acknowledge the LORD;
let us press on to acknowledge him.

---

43  Psalm 27:7-10
44  Psalm 42:1-2
45  Psalm 63:1-2
46  Hosea 4:1

As surely as the sun rises,

he will appear;

he will come to us like the winter rains,

like the spring rains that water the earth."[47]

All of these verses speak of searching, expecting, and hungering for knowledge. Following the examples of David, Hosea, and Asaph, I always told my students that we need to seek the Lord and strive to know Him. However, after my lectures, the head teacher would always correct me; he said that we do not need to seek God because He is with us.

As a graduate of the Dallas Theological Seminary, he held the view of the majority of the Evangelical wing of the church, which says: God has found us, and we have accepted Him; therefore, He is with us. This suggests a logical conclusion: If He is with us, we need not seek Him.

But I always thought, *Then all these verses in the Psalms, Proverbs, and the Prophets don't apply to us? Why, for centuries, were the Psalms a consolation for so many Christians during times of persecution, hunger, cold, rejection, misunderstanding, indifference, and loneliness? If they are not for us, then why are believers still seeking the Lord?*

Yes, Jesus says, "And surely I am with you always, to the very end of the age."[48] But do we really know Him Who is with us?

## FOLLOWING IN OUR FATHERS' FOOTSTEPS

Let us now turn to those who followed Christ many years before us.

Paul, a Pharisee sitting at the feet of Gamaliel—one of the founders of Talmudic Judaism—became the most famous herald of the Gospel—a voice from Heaven who wrote half of the books of the New Testament. Through the prism of his messages, we more deeply and completely understand the teachings of Christ in the Gospels. Paul writes to the Philippine church, "I

---

47   Hosea 6:3
48   Matthew 28:20b

consider everything a loss because of the surpassing worth of knowing Christ Jesus my Lord, for whose sake I have lost all things. I consider them garbage, that I may gain Christ."[49]

Gregory the Theologian, Archbishop of Constantinople and one of the three great Cappadocian Fathers, who preferred the desert to the bishopric, exclaims, "But for me the great wealth is Christ. Oh, if I would ever see Him with a clear, unveiled mind! Let the world possess all the rest!"[50]

Augustine, the great Christian thinker venerated by Protestants, Catholics, and Orthodox alike, proclaims, "Unhappy is the man who knows everything but does not know You; blessed is he who knows You, even if he knows nothing else."[51]

Erasmus of Rotterdam, the forerunner of the Reformation, the Prince of Humanists, the first translator of the Greek New Testament, says, "But when the eyes of your heart have darkened and you don't see the most bright light, which is the truth, when with your inner ear you are not hearing the voice of God, when you have no feelings, then do you think your soul is alive?"[52]

John Calvin, the author of the *Institutes of the Christian Religion*, one of the pillars of the Protestant Reformation, wrote:

> For as long as people do not comprehend properly that they owe everything to God, that they lovingly feed on his father's breast, that in Him is the source of all good, He will not be the sole purpose of their aspirations; until then, they will never arrive at sincere piety. Moreover, if people do not learn to put all their happiness in God, they will never truly and selflessly worship Him.[53]

---

49  Philippians 3:8
50  St. Gregory the Theologian, "To His Soul," in *Spiritual Creations, Instructing the Basics of Life* (Ark Publishing, 2000).
51  St. Augustine, *Confessions* (Metairie: Renaissance Publishing, 1991).
52  Desiderious Erasmus, *The Manual of a Christian Knight*, (Kharkiv: Litera Nova Publishing, 2017).
53  John Calvin, *Institutes of the Christian Religion* (Aslan Publishing, 1997).

In the first half of the twentieth century, Pastor Aiden Tozer, writes:

> Similarly the Presence of God is the central fact of Christianity.
> At the heart of the Christian message is God Himself waiting
> for His redeemed children to push into conscious awareness
> of His Presence. That type of Christianity which happens
> now to be the vogue knows this Presence only in theory. It
> fails to stress the Christian's privilege of present realization.
> According to its teachings we are in the Presence of God
> positionally, and nothing is said about the need to experience
> that Presence actually.[54]

Did our predecessors have a different Bible? Why do we come to different conclusions?

## WHAT IS OUR FAITH?

Let's examine the most important thing that we have—faith. What is our faith? Is it a mental conviction that Jesus is our Savior, that He died for us on the cross, and that we are saved by grace? Is it the mechanical pronouncement of the standard prayer of repentance? "God, forgive me for my sins; please come into my heart; become my Lord; I now accept Jesus as my God and Savior." You can't find this prayer in Scripture. Have you seen people who uttered these words, yet their lives did not change at all? I have certainly witnessed this.

Once, after teaching a course at our regional Bible school, I took a taxi from Bishkek, the capital of Kyrgyzstan, to Almaty. Taxis between the big cities sell individual seats, so many people could share one car. On this particular ride, one of the passengers was a Scotsman. I am always interested in talking to people from other cultures, and we talked about many things and discussed spiritual questions. He considered himself a Christian, though he said that the Bible cannot be completely trusted because not everything written there is from God. He also thought that half of the Quran is God's

---

54   A.W. Tozer, *The Pursuit of God* (Tustin: Loki's Publishing, 2017).

Word, and there is much truth in Buddhism. He also shared about his life. Divorced for many years, he had not seen his children for a long time, but he lives with a girl and pays for her education. He devotes all his time to business, and his only entertainment is a glass of whiskey.

When the driver stopped for a break, we got out of the car and were left alone. I told him that he needed to repent and accept Jesus as his Lord and Savior and receive salvation. He replied, "I don't need to do it again because I have already accepted Jesus as my God and Savior." Then he looked up at sky with tears in his eyes and said, "I am fully confident that the time will come when I will be with God in Heaven."

Looking at him, I thought that even Martin Luther and John Calvin would envy his "faith." The worst thing was that he spoke very sincerely and with all his heart.

A missionary friend has an aunt who lives in the USA. She is a lesbian and for many years has been living with her "spouse" as a "family." Every Christmas, she sends a postcard writing about love and faith in Christ Jesus as her God and Savior. I would not be surprised if she considers herself a devoted disciple of the Lord.

So, what is our faith? Let's look at the Gospels and see what Jesus means by faith.

## THE FAITH OF A CANAANITE WOMAN

A Canaanite woman from that vicinity came to him, crying out, "LORD, Son of David, have mercy on me! My daughter is demon-possessed and suffering terribly."
Jesus did not answer a word. So his disciples came to him and urged him, "Send her away, for she keeps crying out after us."
He answered, "I was sent only to the lost sheep of Israel."

The woman came and knelt before him. "Lord, help me!" she said. He replied, "It is not right to take the children's bread and toss it to the dogs."

"Yes it is, Lord," she said. "Even the dogs eat the crumbs that fall from their master's table."

Then Jesus answered, "Woman, you have great faith! Your request is granted." And her daughter was healed at that moment.[55]

What is this "great faith" that Jesus commended? That she believed in His ability to heal? No. If she didn't believe that, she would not have come to Him at all. She refers to Him as Messiah ("Son of David"). Yet the Savior harasses her twice:

1.   He ignores her. She screamed so loudly and for so long that the disciples supported her request.

2.   He says "cruel" words: "It is not right to take the children's bread and toss it to the dogs." Whom did He call a dog? The woman or her daughter?

Any other person would be offended by Jesus and leave, but she boldly says, "Yes it is, Lord . . . Even the dogs eat the crumbs that fall from the table of their master's table."

Why does Jesus do this to her? Did He want to make fun of her? No. He does it for the sake of the disciples. Like a surgeon during an operation, He draws His students' attention to things they would not normally notice. Through these "harassments," He reveals the power source of great faith: the knowledge that He is good. If someone with a humble heart insists on asking for help, He will not turn away.

### THE FAITH OF THE SINNER

When one of the Pharisees invited Jesus to have dinner with him, he went to the Pharisee's house and reclined at the table. A woman in that town who lived a sinful life learned that Jesus was eating at the Pharisee's house, so she came there with an alabaster jar of perfume. As she stood behind him at his feet

---

55   Matthew 15:22-28

weeping, she began to wet his feet with her tears. Then she wiped them with her hair, kissed them and poured perfume on them.

When the Pharisee who had invited him saw this, he said to himself, "If this man were a prophet, he would know who is touching him and what kind of woman she is—that she is a sinner."

Jesus answered him, "Simon, I have something to tell you."

"Tell me, teacher," he said.

"Two people owed money to a certain moneylender. One owed him five hundred denarii, and the other fifty. Neither of them had the money to pay him back, so he forgave the debts of both. Now which of them will love him more?"

Simon replied, "I suppose the one who had the bigger debt forgiven."

"You have judged correctly," Jesus said.

Then he turned toward the woman and said to Simon, "Do you see this woman? I came into your house. You did not give me any water for my feet, but she wet my feet with her tears and wiped them with her hair. You did not give me a kiss, but this woman, from the time I entered, has not stopped kissing my feet. You did not put oil on my head, but she has poured perfume on my feet. Therefore, I tell you, her many sins have been forgiven—as her great love has shown. But whoever has been forgiven little loves little."

Then Jesus said to her, "Your sins are forgiven."

The other guests began to say among themselves, "Who is this who even forgives sins?"

Jesus said to the woman, "Your faith has saved you; go in peace."[56]

Faith dared to cross the threshold of the Pharisee's house, bringing the dearest thing of all—an alabaster vessel filled with myrrh. Faith wiped the feet of the Lord with its hair.

We see the act, but what is under the surface? Her faith revealed her love for God, Who is capable of accepting a repentant sinner.

## THE FAITH OF THE SAMARITAN LEPER

Now on his way to Jerusalem, Jesus traveled along the border between Samaria and Galilee. As he was going into a village, ten men who had leprosy met him. They stood at a distance and called out in a loud voice, "Jesus, Master, have pity on us!"

When he saw them, he said, "Go, show yourselves to the priests." And as they went, they were cleansed.

One of them, when he saw he was healed, came back, praising God in a loud voice. He threw himself at Jesus' feet and thanked him—and he was a Samaritan.

Jesus asked, "Were not all ten cleansed? Where are the other nine? Has no one returned to give praise to God except this foreigner?" Then he said to him, "Rise and go; your faith has made you well."[57]

When the Samaritan saw what happened to him, he turned back, and his heart, overflowing with gratitude, did not hide its joy as he fell at the feet of the Lord. Peel back a layer of the leper's faith, and what do we see underneath? Glory given to Him Who is worthy.

## THE FAITH OF THE CENTURION

When Jesus had entered Capernaum, a centurion came to him, asking for help.

"Lord," he said, "my servant lies at home paralyzed, suffering terribly."

Jesus said to him, "Shall I come and heal him?"

The centurion replied, "Lord, I do not deserve to have you come under my roof. But just say the word, and my servant will be healed. For I myself am a man under authority, with soldiers under me. I tell this one, 'Go,' and he goes; and that one, 'Come,' and he comes. I say to my servant, 'Do this,' and he does it."

---

57  Luke 17:11-19

> When Jesus heard this, he was amazed and said to those following him, "Truly I tell you, I have not found anyone in Israel with such great faith."[58]

What hides behind the faith that surprised Jesus? Basically, the centurion says to Jesus, "I am a man who is in submission, and I have some power. But You are the One Who has all power. Why should You go to my house?" The centurion understands Who is before him. This faith surprised Jesus. During the Transfiguration, the disciples closest to Christ—Peter, James, and John—ask Jesus, "Why then do the teachers of the law say that Elijah must come first?" After reading their question, we begin to see that up until that time, the disciples did not yet have a complete understanding of Jesus as Messiah. Only after they see the glory of Christ, after they see Jesus speak to Moses and Elijah, after they hear a Voice from the cloud saying, "This is my Son, in whom I love; with him, I am well pleased"—only then are they sure that Jesus is Who He says He is.[59] The centurion understood at the beginning what the disciples understood only at the end.

Everyone knows the story when the Lord slept in a boat and a storm arose. They wake Him up and ask for help. Having calmed the wind, He says to them: "Where is your faith?" In other words, "Do you still not understand Who is with you?"

Faith is not just some kind of mental conviction, self-assurance, or confidence. The root of true faith is in God as He is. Faith arises from our understanding of His nature: His mercy, His goodness, His holiness, His greatness. By learning more about His character, His will, and His ways, our faith becomes stronger and stronger.

---

58  Matthew 8: 5-10
59  Matthew 17:1-13

## THE LOST CABOOSE

In the booklet *Have You Heard of the Four Spiritual Laws?*, there is an illustration of a train composed of a locomotive, a car, and a caboose. The locomotive is Fact; the car is Faith; and the caboose is Feelings.[60] In our Spiritual Growth course at seminary, Campus Crusade's leaders reiterated that God must be accepted by faith based on facts, not feelings. I agree with this; feelings come after faith. However, in evangelical Christianity, the caboose broke away from the train and was left to rot in the middle of the steppe.

In conservative Christianity, faith dreads feelings, like an obedient boy who sees the local bully and hides behind a fence. Our faith adores facts, logic, study, discipline, and principles and fears anything unknown, secret, immeasurable, uncontrollable, and incomprehensible. Our faith is guarded by facts and logic. As soon as these guards hear the footsteps of the heart, they raise up their spears and force it away.

Let's open the Scriptures and see what God has to say:

**MATTHEW**

> Jesus replied: "'Love the Lord your God with all your heart and with all your soul and with all your mind.' This is the first and greatest commandment. And the second is like it: 'Love your neighbor as yourself.' All the Law and the Prophets hang on these two commandments" (Matt. 22:37-40).

---

60   From *Have You Heard of the Four Spiritual Laws?* written by Bill Bright, ©1965-2021 The Bright Media Foundation and Campus Crusade for Christ, Inc. All rights reserved. https://crustores.org/four-laws-english. Included by permission.

### MARK

One of the teachers of the law came and heard them debating. Noticing that Jesus had given them a good answer, he asked him, "Of all the commandments, which is the most important?"

"The most important one," answered Jesus, "is this: 'Hear, O Israel, the Lord our God, the Lord is one. Love the Lord your God with all your heart and with all your soul and with all your mind and with all your strength.' The second is this: 'Love your neighbor as yourself.' There is no commandment greater than these" (Mark 12: 28-31).

### LUKE

On one occasion an expert in the law stood up to test Jesus. "Teacher," he asked, "what must I do to inherit eternal life?"

"What is written in the Law?" he replied. "How do you read it?"

He answered: "'Love the Lord your God with all your heart and with all your soul and with all your strength and with all your mind'; and, 'Love your neighbor as yourself'" (Luke 10:25-27).

Matthew, Mark, and Luke put *mind* at the end and the heart first. We have surrendered the heart to the mercy of the mind.

We want to know God through the mind—thinking, logic, learning, facts, research—and through strength—obedience, discipline, work, energy, willpower. But where is the heart, with its mystery, emotions, passion, spontaneity, romance, and creativity? Because feelings are not substantial, our faith battles with them, but it was not always so. This is a consequence of the Fall. But in spite of this inconstancy, why shouldn't we take a risk? Don't we take risks when we go on a date, declare our love, or write a song?

We eventually get married, have children. Let's do the same and take a chance with God. We need to find that caboose, clean out the dust and dirt, and hook it to the locomotive.

## KNOWLEDGE AND SANCTIFICATION

It is important to understand the difference between knowledge and sanctification—at least, the way we often think of sanctification (of course, everything is written correctly in theological books). Knowledge is a very important word for me. In Russian, we have two words: Знание Бога and Познание Бога. Знание Бога means "knowledge of God," as in a more theoretical knowledge of God like reading the Bible or Christian books about God; I know *about God*. Познание Бога means "knowing God" by having a deep connection with Him; I am *experiencing* Him. In modern Christianity, sanctification is defined by following commandments: I am sanctified if I don't curse, don't steal, don't drink, don't start a fight, and if I attend church, tithe, and preach the Gospel. Often, in our idea sanctification, everything begins with man's effort.

In a true knowledge of God, everything begins with God. We need to understand the nature of our obedience. Do I do good by virtue of my will, discipline, or a checkmark in my diary? Or do I do good because I understand the forgiveness and love of God and want to extend that to another person? True sanctification should lead us to the glorification of God, not to the exaltation of man.

## I AM GOOD ENOUGH

However, there *are* people who understand the importance of truly knowing God. They also read Brent Curtis and John Eldridge's *The Sacred Romance*, John Piper's *Desiring God*, and James Packer's *Knowing God*. Yet why is there no progress?

In my current job in the Human Resources department of a pharmaceutical company, I am involved in the hiring process. One of the key criteria for hiring an employee is experience. We assume that the more the candidate has worked at a similar position, the more professional he should be.

However, after working for many years in the company, I will say that this is not entirely true. What do we read in a resumé? That the candidate spent four years at Novartis. But the resumé does not say *how* he spent those years at Novartis. It is important to know how the employee developed at the company.

Regardless of the position (medical representative, accountant, or logistics), the same is often true; just look at this chart:

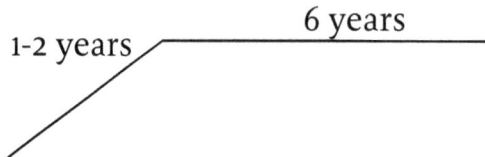

A person actively grows during the first one or two years in a company: new position, new responsibilities which require new skills, new environment. After a while, though, the person looks around and thinks, "I'm basically no worse than others and maybe even better. I do everything that's required of me." He enters the so-called "comfort zone." Then he just does the same thing over and over, and no growth is observed.

The same happens with believers. At first, a person is "on fire." The new believer comes to the morning service, remains for the afternoon service, and wonders why others do not do the same. He reads the Bible in several translations and dreams of learning ancient Greek. He tries to share God's message with his neighbors. He leaves the home group later than everyone and then only when the hosts are getting ready for bed. He approaches the elders and, looking into their eyes, earnestly asks their views on Calvinism and Arminianism. Then later, after some amount of time, most people look around and say, "I'm basically no worse than others and maybe even better. I don't smoke, don't drink, don't commit adultery. I tithe; I serve; I read the Bible."

Is this the future God has prepared for us?

When Abram was ninety-nine years old, the LORD appeared to him and said, "I am God Almighty; walk before me and be blameless. Then I will make my covenant between me and you and will greatly increase your numbers."

Abram fell facedown, and God said to him, "As for me, this is my covenant with you: You will be the father of many nations. No longer will you be called Abram; your name will be Abraham, for I have made you a father of many nations. I will make you very fruitful; I will make nations of you, and kings will come from you. I will establish my covenant as an everlasting covenant between me and you and your descendants after you for the generations to come, to be your God and the God of your descendants after you. The whole land of Canaan, where you are now a foreigner, I will give as an everlasting possession to you and your descendants after you; and I will be their God.[61]

God gives Abraham a great future. He gives him a new name. He wants to take him to a new level. But how does Abraham react to this? "Abraham said to God, 'If only Ishmael might live under your blessing!'"[62]

Abraham only cares about keeping what he already has. This is his "comfort zone." But God always wants something more for us. He wants us to ask and seek for more. Sometimes, even when He doesn't require it of us, He wants us to press on for more.

Now Elisha had been suffering from the illness from which he died. Jehoash king of Israel went down to see him and wept over him. "My father! My father!" he cried. "The chariots and horsemen of Israel!"

Elisha said, "Get a bow and some arrows," and he did so. "Take the bow in your hands," he said to the king of Israel. When he had taken it, Elisha put his hands on the king's hands.

"Open the east window," he said, and he opened it. "Shoot!" Elisha said, and he shot. "The LORD's arrow of victory, the arrow

---

61   Genesis 17:1-8
62   Genesis 17:18

of victory over Aram!" Elisha declared. "You will completely destroy the Arameans at Aphek."

Then he said, "Take the arrows," and the king took them. Elisha told him, "Strike the ground." He struck it three times and stopped. The man of God was angry with him and said, "You should have struck the ground five or six times; then you would have defeated Aram and completely destroyed it. But now you will defeat it only three times."[63]

There, at the end of the passage, I'm surprised by Elisha's anger. What was Jehoash's fault? The prophet told him to take the arrows and hit them on the ground. He did not instruct him to take the arrows and hit the ground six times. If he had said that, would the king have dared to disobey?

An interpretation comes to me: it is God's will that we desire more. He wants us to take the initiative, to make it a part of our character. The character of Jehoash was to hit the ground just three times.

In the course "Bible Study Methods," we were taught that the narrative genre is divided into three types: dramas, reports, and speeches. The fourth chapter of the first book of Chronicles is a typical example of a narrative report. The descendants of Judah are listed there—who is the father, who is the son, who is the wife, etc. In verses nine and ten, however, the author departs from the usual style of presentation and writes: "Jabez was more honorable than his brothers. His mother had named him Jabez, saying, 'I gave birth to him in pain.' Jabez cried out to the God of Israel, 'Oh, that you would bless me and enlarge my territory! Let your hand be with me, and keep me from harm so that I will be free from pain.' And God granted his request."[64]

Who do we want to be? Number 386 on page 120, or those about whom they say, "And God granted his request."

---

63  2 Kings 13:14-19
64  1 Chronicles 4:9-10

CHAPTER 6

# IN SEARCH OF THE WHISPERING WIND

THE BEGGAR WOMAN RECOGNIZED HER lost son, but the Star Boy chased her away and later turned into a monster.

> So he went to the well of water and looked into it, and lo! his face was as the face of a toad, and his body was sealed like an adder. . . . And there came to him the little daughter of the Woodcutter, and she put her hand upon his shoulder and said, "What doth it matter if thou hast lost thy comeliness? Stay with us, and I will not mock at thee." And he said to her, "Nay, but I have been cruel to my mother, and as a punishment has this evil been sent to me. Wherefore I must go hence, and wander through the world till I find her, and she give me her forgiveness."[65]

He ran along the forest road, calling and begging his mother to come back. The Star Boy went in search of his mother. We need to search for the Father. However, we need to know the direction in which to go.

In the previous chapter, we talked about what hinders us; now, let's talk about what will help us.

## GOD IS ALL IN ALL

Corporate trainers and coaches use a variety of tools to help increase employee efficiency. One of the most popular is called the Wheel of Life. Here is an example:

---

65  Wilde, ibid.

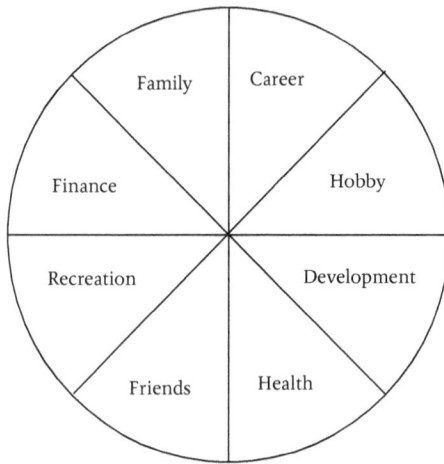

Each area is labeled as a sphere of your life. For example, family, career, hobby, finance, health, friends, recreation, and development. Then you rate each spoke on a scale from zero (the axle) to ten (the rim). Recently, another area has emerged that was previously absent: spiritual. Everyone understands this sphere differently depending on their religion or belief system, but many thought it was important enough to add to the wheel in addition to finance, career, and recreation.

However, for disciples of Christ, a relationship with God cannot be merely one part of the total package, just one of the spokes in the wheel. For us, God is All in all. The apostle Paul wrote to the Colossians, "All things have been created through him and for him."[66] And then he encouraged them to "set your minds on things above, not on the earthly things. For you died, and your life is now hidden with Christ in God."[67] Because he believed that God is All in all, Paul made himself a sacrifice.[68] Likewise, David refused to make a sacrifice that was no cost to himself, so he paid Araunah both for the threshing floor and for the oxen.[69]

---

66   Colossians 1:16
67   Colossians 3:3
68   Romans 12:1
69   2 Samuel 24:18-25

Can we say, "I have a three-story house; my business brings in millions; my ministry is growing; my spouse loves me; and the children are healthy; but if my heart is not seeking God, then all the rest is rubbish"?

Mikhail Romm, the famous Soviet documentarian and director of the film *Ordinary Fascism*, expressed something similar to Jesus as the Amen in the book of Revelation: "Cinema should be either cold or hot. Only garbage is warm."

Are we on fire for God? Is our heart torn from our chest? Are we seeking Him more than anything else?

From a preacher's perspective, I have my own thoughts on what the highest disregard of God is. I spend days preparing a sermon in the evening after a hard day's work, doing exegetical and homiletical analysis, writing an introduction revealing a need (according to Haddon Robinson), assessing it based on Christo-centricity (according to John Piper), defining a focus, breaking it into points, reading commentaries in Russian and English, and researching phrases in Greek and Hebrew. All this is done so that in the middle of the sermon, a parishioner should collect her things and say that she needs to go. After all, we have a meeting every week, but the opening of a McDonald's is once in a lifetime.

I caught myself doing the same thing. I shared with a pastor friend, "You know, if you remove Christ, my preaching wouldn't change. Yes, I talk about things like being salt and light, how to raise children, how to preach the Gospel, how to do good, but Christ is not in it. It's possible to say the word 'Christ' three hundred times in a sermon, yet Christ will not be there."

We can easily turn from Christianity into a Tony Robbins, a famous motivational speaker. How shall we make God our All in all? Hear the words of Christ: "No one can serve two masters. Either you will hate the one and love the other, or you will be devoted to the one and despise the other."[70]

---

70   Matthew 6:24

At the beginning of my full-time ministry, I could not make quiet time a part of my life. At first, I didn't have enough time; then I got lazy; then I forgot. When I came to the end of my rope, I made a decision: If I do not spend time with God today, I will consider that day spent in vain. Despite anything else that happens during the day—preparing for a sermon, leading a home group, or spending time with my wife—all is in vain. And vice versa: If I spend time with God and do nothing else, then that day is super successful.

It helped, for a time. Unfortunately, quiet time—or, more precisely, how we spend our quiet time—can become a comfort zone, even an obstacle to a relationship with God. How is this possible?

Every time I heard or read about knowing God, I thought, *This doesn't concern me. I have a quiet time, and therefore, everything is in order.* It even became a source of secret pride. Then I realized that my quiet time didn't bring me closer to God. My quiet time had become too practical. It resembled a grocery shopping list. It was just a list of needs.

I said, "God, thank You that You are kind and loving. Thank You for giving Your Son for us," and a few more things like that. Next came the list:

- God, bless me and my family today.
- God, help me prepare the sermon.
- God, we still don't have our own home; help us in this.
- God, my parents are coming to visit; please protect them on their way.
- God, repair the car.
- God, a brother in church lost his job; please help him.
- God, heal my child.
- God, bless our service on Sunday.

And so on . . .

I realized that the theme of my quiet time was, "God, what can You do for me today?" A true relationship with God is based on the theme, "God, Who are You?"

Now I try to talk to God about Him—about His heart, His Mercy, His Love, His Kingdom, His plans. I talk to Him about things I don't understand. When I make requests, it is more about learning to distinguish His voice from my own and learning to obey Him. Yes, I have needs, but they don't come first. I don't mean to say that you shouldn't ask God about your needs. Yes, you should, and this will also be spiritual. But if this is all we talk about, then our relationship will become like buyer and Seller, in which prayer is the currency, and the Seller should promptly respond.

We must seek God following the example of Jonathan, who loved David so much that he gave him his clothes, a sword, a bow, and a belt. It is written that "Jonathan became one in spirit with David."[71] May our souls cleave to the Lord.

## COME TO GOD AS YOU ARE

When I get cut off on the road, I angrily chase the driver to do the same to him or shout insults. I scold my wife for buying new shoes because her seven-year-old pair are still wearable. I talk to my colleagues more gently than to my children. I seek justice more than mercy. This is what lies in the recesses of my heart. This I must bring to God.

Many years ago, I heard a preacher say, "You need not preach to God; you need only to open your heart." In sermons, I say, "If you have no desire to pray, then pray about it. Come to the Father and tell Him you have no desire to pray, or no desire to know Him, or no desire to read the Word, but do not stop there. Ask God to fill your heart with a thirst for Him."

There is no other way. Come to Him as you are.

Any other way is hypocrisy.

## EAR SURGERY

I have a friend, Alexander, who is one of the best ear, nose, and throat surgeons in the country. He operated on my nose. Recently, when I asked him about

---

his surgeries, he replied that the nose is his least favorite. "I want to learn new skills, so I mostly work with the ear because it is a much more complicated organ."

This intrigued me, so I asked, "How do people lose their hearing?"

"Injuries, infections . . . "

"If an eardrum bursts, what do you do?"

"I cut tissue from inside the ear—tissue similar in structure to the eardrum—and I make a new one. Then the person can hear again."

It would be great if there were such a thing for believers, and I suppose many believers would want this operation if it were possible. Why? Because trying to know God without being able to hear Him is the same as trying to play tennis without a racket.

Unfortunately, the ability to hear God is a more complicated process. To learn to hear God, you must first believe that this is possible. Not all Christians believe that you can talk with God. They believe in the kind of prayer where a person speaks and God listens. They do not expect God to answer. Some believe that God speaks but don't fervently seek to hear Him, so this is basically the same thing.

The Evangelical tradition holds that after the church received the Bible, God no longer addressed His people directly. The *Westminster Confession of Faith*, Chapter 1, "Of the Holy Scripture," Point 1 reads:

> Therefore it pleased the Lord, at sundry times, and in divers manners, to reveal Himself, and to declare that His will unto His Church; and afterwards, for the better preserving and propagating of the truth, and for the more sure establishment and comfort of the Church against the corruption of the flesh, and the malice of Satan and of the world, to commit the same wholly unto writing: which maketh the Holy Scripture to be most necessary; those former ways of God's revealing His will unto His people being now ceased.[72]

---

72 "Chapter 1 - Of the Holy Scripture," *Westminster Confession of Faith*, Crown and Covenant Church.org, http://crowncovenantchurch.org/confessions/WestminsterCOF.aspx?QuestionID=1&pageid=0&confession=true&q=Chapter+1+-+Of+the+Holy+Scripture (accessed October 14, 2020).

Jack Deere, author and former professor at Dallas Theological Seminary, works to prove that miracles, healings, and the ability to communicate directly with God are not a thing of the past. In his book *Surprised by the Power of the Holy Spirit*, he writes, "If you were to lock a brand new Christian in a room with a Bible and tell him to study what Scripture has to say about healing and miracles, he would never come out of the room a cessationist."[73]

I am an example of that. When I became a believer, there were twenty people in our church, all former Muslims with a communist past. In the city of three hundred thousand people, there were four or five churches with a total of no more than 150 members. Naturally, we did not have any traditions. There was no Christian shop or Bible school in the region. I did not have a single piece of Christian literature besides the Bible and a few tracts.

At that time, my pastor, Yerlan, had been a believer for only three years. A missionary had preached the Gospel, baptized him, and left. Subsequently, Yerlan and his family began the meeting. Therefore, he taught us what he read in the Bible.

By reading the Scripture, we believed that God heals, works miracles, and speaks to us. Later, in the seminary, I was told that my teaching was not entirely biblical and that I needed to be done with miracles.

One of the clearest testimonies of the first year of my conversion occurred when I worked at a trading company as a forwarding agent, a person who executes orders by the trading team. We transported food before lunch and then returned to the office to eat and await further orders. One afternoon, I had a desire to go to the city center, a desire so strong that I could not sit still. I had to go. Of course, I had to find a reason, and I told myself that there was a good bookstore there. Having walked a couple of kilometers, I thought, *What am I doing? I don't have time to get there and back.* So, I turned around.

---

73   Jack Deere, *Surprised by the Power of the Spirit: Discovering How God Speaks and Heals Today* (Grand Rapids: Zondervan Academic, 1996).

At that very moment, I heard someone calling my name. "Kanat, Kanat." Looking in the direction of the voice, next to a telephone box, I saw Kuat, a youth ministry leader from a neighboring town whom I had met at a Christian camp. He approached me. "Listen, I have some business in your city and need a place to spend the night. I called you and Ruslan, but no one answered. I don't know your address. So, I sat down and began to pray. I lifted my head and saw you coming."

As I reflect on this, I understand it was no accident. I should not have been in that place at that time. I was there because something called me. I had not heard a voice, only felt a prompting. That moment taught me that God can do amazing things.

While working at the mission, we were continually taught that God does not speak directly to us, though He can speak through a pastor or another believer. Some missionaries used this method. If they needed an answer to an important question, they would pray. If they felt anxiety, they thought it was not of God. But if they felt peace and joy, it was of God. Yet even then, they did not say that God was speaking to them. The ministers were very cautious if someone came and said, "God told me . . . " When we saw the word "prophet" in the New Testament, we interpreted it as a "preacher."[74] This then raised the question, how does a prophet differ from a teacher? In time, I replaced hearing God with exegetical and hermeneutic analysis of the text.

Teaching the course "Methods of Bible Study: Genre Narration" for many years, I had a question that I couldn't get out of my head. I used various Scriptural examples during the course, including Joshua chapter nine. It tells how the Gibeonites tricked the Israelites. God gave Israel the promised land and commanded them to destroy the nations living there. The inhabitants of Gibeon decided to make an alliance with Israel. At first, the Israelis did not want to conclude a treaty and said, "But perhaps you live near us, so how can

---

we make a treaty with you?"[75] But the Gibeonites said they came from a far country and showed moldy bread and worn out clothes. Then, "The Israelites sampled their provisions but did not inquire of the LORD."[76]

The study of the passage is built on three levels:

1. Observation—What do we see?
2. Interpretation—What does this mean?
3. Application—How do we bring to into practice?

Considering the application, several principles can be found. But the most important one could be, "When making key decisions, you need to ask God and not rely on your mind." This would be a wonderful application for that time when God spoke directly with His people. The kings had prophets. But I thought, *How does the passage relate to modern times?*

After completing my work with the mission, I often thought about the ninth chapter of Joshua. I read books on the topic of hearing God. *How to Listen to God* by Charles Stanley, *Surprised by the Voice of God* by Jack Deere, and *The Voice of God* by Cindy Jacobs. I realized that an important step in hearing God is the ability to discern the voice of God.

A believer can hear three voices: the voice of God, his own voice, and the voice of the enemy. The hardest thing is to distinguish the voice of God from your own voice. The voice of the enemy is easiest to distinguish, provided you know the Bible well. He is loud, proud, independent, and speaks in a voice contrary to the Spirit of Scripture.

In 2011, I left the mission and attempted to start my own training company. It didn't work out, so I went looking for a job. But that didn't work out either. For almost a year, I was completely unemployed. I sat in the kitchen and listened to the voice of the enemy: "Finally, you understand that you are a

---

75   Joshua 9:7
76   Joshua 9:14

nobody. What have you spent your best years on? Who needs your ten years of experience in the mission? You'll go to Procter & Gamble and say that you have taught Bible study methods for the last ten years. Who needs a Kazakh Christian in a Muslim country? Look at your fellow students; they got worse grades than you, and now they drive a Lexus and take vacations in Bali. Some are interviewed on TV. And look at yourself; soon you'll be forty years old, and it's hard for you to pay rent or even afford a coat for your wife."

In the midst of this tirade, I heard a quiet Voice say, "Pray for a new car." This was not my thought. I didn't have enough money for gas. I didn't know if my family would eat tomorrow. When my wife said that our daughter had grown and needed new shoes, I asked several times to put the shoes on her feet and check whether they really were too small.

Since I had determined that I would not only learn to hear the voice of God but also obey Him, I made myself get up from my chair. In front of the refrigerator, I made the shortest prayer in my life. "God, give me a new car. Amen." I immediately forgot about this "stupid" prayer.

I lost all hope of finding work, so I went back to my failed business. When somebody bought a training course, then we had a little money, which I tried to stretch for several months. Then I received a letter from a recruiting company to which I had sent my resumé more than a year earlier. I read, "Dear Kanat. We found your resume in our database and want to inform you that a large pharmaceutical company is looking for a training manager. Could you suggest someone for this position, or perhaps this position might interest you?"

A few days later, I was hired, despite the huge number of applicants. I was offered a salary five times the national average. I turned out to be one of just a few employees without a medical education. At the end of the interview, my new boss said, "The person in your position must have a car. In a few days, you will receive it." At that moment, I heard a quiet Voice say, "Now do you understand why I asked you to pray for the car?"

You might think this story is about the car. But as I reflect on that period of my life, I think it was about something else. I would preach on Sunday about the hope that God gives, and then after church, I would pass a supermarket and envy the people leaving it with bags full of groceries. No, the Voice was not talking about the car at all. He was saying, "I am with you." And now I can say the same as Jacob, "Surely the LORD is in this place, and I was not aware of it."[77] I did not merely read about it; I lived it.

In Evangelical Christianity, a controversial situation is taking shape, similar to the one I encountered a couple of years ago. I bought a plot of land in the mountains and received permission to build a house, but all the roads to the mountains had signs: "No Trucks Allowed." How am I going to transport steel reinforcement twenty feet long or two hundred tons of concrete? In my pocket?

So, here it is. We are told that having a complete Bible, God no longer directly speaks to people, and the prophetic gift does not exist. At the same time, we teach that prayer is a conversation with God—not a monologue, but a dialogue with God. It seems to me the very idea that God cannot communicate directly with a believer destroys the very possibility of knowing God.

## IN THE LIBRARY OF GOD

As a child, I loved going to the library. I liked everything about it: a two-story building with peeling plaster, creaking stairs to the second floor, the librarian behind the counter with his head down, no need to say hello to anyone. The most important thing in the library is silence. I would go to the shelves and take a book, leaf through it, read something, put it back in place, and take another. This was my kingdom—shelves to the ceiling, tattered bindings, letters on paper. Oh, and the smell of the library. The older the book, the more delicious it smelled.

---

77   Genesis 28:16

God has His own library. The most important book is the Bible. From its pages, you will sense the hint of a whispering wind. Preachers call us to read the Bible; the Bible calls us to meditate on the Bible:

> Blessed is the one
> who does not walk in step with the wicked
> or stand in the way that sinners take
> or sit in the company of mockers.
> but whose delight is in the law of the LORD,
> and who meditates on his law day and night.[78]

> "Be strong and very courageous. Be careful to obey all the law my servant Moses gave you; do not turn from it to the right or to the left, that you may be successful wherever you go. Keep this Book of the Law depart always on your lips; meditate on it day and night, so that you may be careful to do everything written in it. Then you will be prosperous and successful."[79]

> I meditate on your precepts
> and consider your ways.[80]

> Though rulers sit together and slander me,
> your servant will meditate on your decrees.[81]

> Oh, how I love your law!
> I meditate on it all day long.[82]

> I have more insight than all my teachers,
> for I meditate on your statutes.[83]

---

78   Psalms 1:1-2
79   Joshua 1:7-8
80   Psalm 119:15
81   Psalm 119:23
82   Psalm 119:97
83   Psalm 119:99

If we desire fellowship with the whispering wind, just reading the text is not enough; we need to meditate on the Word of God.

Yes, we live in the era of fast food Christianity; we have no time. We must ask ourselves if God is really All in all for us because reading without meditating is meaningless. It is better to reflect on three verses than to read three chapters and forget them before you reach the garage.

I think time should be divided in this way: thirty percent reading and seventy percent thinking. In the process of reflection, you again and again return to the passage. While meditating, pray and ask God to reveal the Word to you. The ability to hear God will help. It will also help if you are proficient in Bible study, if you know a lot about different genres, and if you have read Gordon Fee and Howard Hendricks. And it's better if you meditate on the Word throughout the day.

Suppose you spend quiet time in the morning but need to be at the office at nine o'clock. You may find it difficult to meditate on the Word under limited conditions. Divide your quiet time into two parts: morning—dedicated to prayer—and evening—meditating on the Word. One other benefit is that you start the day with God and end with God.

Why do I say this to missionaries and ministers? Because I myself am a minister, and I know that many of us never even think about Scripture unless we need to prepare for a sermon, a study group, or a conference. We spend more time studying systematic theology, commentaries, and reference books.

Some fear that direct contact with God will lead to the rejection of the authority of Scripture. Never! On the contrary, the Bible gives us the understanding of God's voice. The better we hear God, the greater our desire to study the Scriptures. The more we study the Scripture, the better we hear our God.

I like reading biographies. They are written by biographers who have observed the life of the person about whom they are writing. But the most interesting books are autobiographies or letters left by the person himself.

In the same way, the Bible is an autobiography—a book about Him, written by Himself.

Scripture and hearing God complement each other, like a ship and a mast with a sail. The Scripture talks about the calling of an apostle (a missionary); the Spirit of God says to which country one should go, Kenya or Mongolia. The Scripture says how spouses should relate: "Wives, submit yourselves to your own husbands as you do to the Lord. . . Husbands, love your wives, just as Christ loved the church and gave himself up for her."[84] However very few of us run to read the Bible when we quarrel with our spouse, but a gentle Voice says, "Go and ask for forgiveness, even if you consider yourself in the right. Your spouse is My gift to you."

## MORE THAN A SPECTATOR

Have you ever thought about the popularity of television shows like *The X Factor* and *America's Got Talent*? In my opinion, first of all, it's interesting to observe how people fulfill their dreams right in front of our eyes. Second, it gives hope that we, too, could do this. We used to think of Salvador Dali or Luciano Pavarotti as geniuses. But when we see Melanie Amaro, nineteen years old and from an ordinary family, or Landau Eugene Murphy, Jr., a thirty-six-year-old car washer, succeed in great ways, then we have hope that we can, too. All this observation does not help us achieve our dreams; that's the worst of it. We just continue to watch other people's victories.

This also applies to believers. Turning to Scripture, we see David defeating Goliath, Elijah calling fire from heaven, and Paul preaching in the public squares. Turning to the history of the church, we see Martin Luther nailing his Ninety-five Theses to the door of the Wittenberg church, Spurgeon organizing a college, and C. S. Lewis writing *The Chronicles of Narnia*. We consider them heroes of faith. The Bible says they were ordinary people. "Elijah was a human being, even as we are. He prayed earnestly that it would

---

IN SEARCH OF THE WHISPERING WIND   87

not rain, and it did not rain on the land for three and a half years."[85] Maybe it's time to stop being mere readers?

How do we do that? Every day, God calls us to something. The question is, how do we respond to this call? It could be something big—go to Syria as a doctor, leave your job and start a business, build a seminary. Or it could be something small: —You were invited to a leadership conference in Honolulu, Hawaii (with all expenses paid), but instead of going yourself, you decided to send a staff member. Or let's say you were in a hurry to get home and saw someone whose car wouldn't start, so you helped and lost an hour of your time, guaranteeing you'll get stuck in traffic. You decide to share the Gospel with a stranger wearing headphones working on a computer in the lobby of a hotel.

Ask yourself, "What one step of faith can I take today? What is God calling me to do today?" In order to truly open your heart, open your mind, and direct all your thoughts to the Eternal, just thinking about the Word and prayer will not be enough. God is inextricably linked with action.

Do not confuse a step of faith with risk or leaving your comfort zone. Risk occurs when the result of an action is both ambiguous and not obvious; there may be several different outcomes, including negative ones, associated with this or that loss. A comfort zone is an area of living space that gives a feeling of comfort and security. To leave the comfort zone means to do something new and unusual, and this is often associated with discomfort and pain.

The footsteps of faith are a response to the guidance of the Holy Spirit. In both risk and leaving the comfort zone, the initiative comes from the individual. In a step of faith, the initiative comes from God. Therefore, if you are a missionary in Afghanistan on your own initiative, you have not taken a step of faith. You should call it either a risk or a step out of your comfort zone. In other words, a step of faith can involve risk and leaving your comfort zone,

---

but both of them are not necessary to be a step of faith. A believer can take a risk and leave his comfort zone; a non-believer cannot make a step of faith because one must be led by the Holy Spirit in order to do so.

My wife, Dinara, never purposefully prayed for healing and did not believe that God could heal people through her prayers. One day, she received a word from the Lord to pray for the boy who lived next door, who had a severe form of cerebral palsy. But she was afraid of how it would look. In Kazakhstan, neighbors go to each other to borrow salt or loan chairs when guests come, but to come and pray for healing is very strange. Even more, she was afraid of what it would look like if she prayed and nothing happened. She did not dare and did not go.

After that, when we moved to another area, she again received a word that she needed to pray for her cousin Mukhit. He was in a very difficult period of life and had no money; because of this, he had a nervous breakdown, which resulted in half of his face being paralyzed. He went for treatment, took the prescribed medication, had injections and physical therapy. After the doctors tried everything they could think of, he was told that his face would remain as it was. He didn't give up and visited traditional healers, which also did not help.

This time, Dinara decided to obey. When we arrived, her cousin met us in the courtyard; he looked like Gwynplaine.[86] Part of his mouth would not close. We talked about the latest news; then Dinara told her sister-in-law that she wanted to pray for her cousin. He sat down on a chair in the corridor, and she prayed in the name of Isa Masih,[87] and he said, "Amen." Then we forgot about it.

A month later, Dinara's mom said in a conversation, "You know, Mukhit's sickness is gone." After that, not only Dinara's faith but also my faith in healing increased, even though I did not pray or lay hands on him. But I saw his face and was in the next room.

---

86  A grotesque character in Victor Hugo's *The Man Who Laughed*
87  The Turkic name for Jesus

Like Peter, we need to get out of the boat. One could say, "Peter almost drowned!" I say, it is better to step out and drown than not to go at all. I am sure when Peter re-entered the boat, he coldly sat with water dripping off him, his heart pounding with fright, while the disciples taunted him. Yet I imagine him smiling.

You can live a kilometer from the ocean and spend time watching *National Geographic* but never get wet. It's time to get out of the house and go to the ocean.

## TWO CROSSES

There are two crosses. One cross belongs to God; the second He has prepared for us. Jesus says, "Whoever does not take up their cross and follow me is not worthy of me."[88] The knowledge of any single quality of God— whether it is His mercy, holiness, love, intimacy, or greatness—will lead us to the cross of Christ. He is holy; therefore, He cannot put up with our sin. He loves us; therefore, He accepted punishment for us. He wanted to be close to us, so He became a man. In His greatness, He was the first to reach out to us.

There is another cross, one that helps us to know God better. It allows us, even for a little while, to walk the path that our Lord walked "for it has been granted to you on behalf of Christ not only to believe in Him, but also to suffer for him."[89] This is the path of suffering and sacrifice.

This is not popular in the age of comfort and personal freedom. Suffering is the forbidden theme of the modern Evangelical church, where favorite topics include financial independence, success, potential, personal growth, family, and conflict resolution. Modern preachers are no different from motivational speakers, except that from time to time, they insert the words "God" and "Jesus."

We find man at the center of sermons in many modern churches. Each sermon tells how man can get help from God. How can God help man to

88  Matthew 10:38
89  Philippians 1:29

save his marriage? How can God help man make more money? How can God fulfill man's goals? In essence, this is the *glorification of man*.

At the center of a biblical sermon stands God. A biblical sermon focuses on glorifying God, knowing God, and expanding His Kingdom. How can we make God the center of our family? How can we obtain God's wisdom regarding the use of finances to expand His Kingdom? How can God's goals become my goals?

Modern prophets say that if someone tells you about your sin, this is not from God; God only speaks of love, mercy, and forgiveness. They claim He does not care about your sins; He came to give health, happiness, and prosperity. Such churches do not focus on sin, on purification through suffering, or excommunication. Some leaders of such churches even try to manipulate the name of God. "Brothers and sisters, I want to prophesy to you that a severe financial crisis is coming to America; but now we will pass the offering plates, and God will protect those who donate and support our ministry. He will not let this crisis touch you. Therefore, give generously— according to your faith, it will be given! And let all the people say 'Hallelujah!'" Then we find out that some of these "anointed ones" use money intended for the ministry to buy planes and build luxury houses. But that's another story.

The cross of Christ deprives man of glory. The cross of Christ leads us to understand that we have nothing to be proud of and find nothing good in ourselves. In the Muslim environment, it is difficult for people to accept the great God dying on a cross. They ask, "What is wrong with this God?" But the cross asks another question: "What is wrong with people?" Did the rags of the beggar woman and her bleeding feet prove that something was wrong with the mother of the Star Boy? Or were they evidence that her love was so great that in spite of pain and suffering, day and night, she sought for her boy.

True knowledge and experience of God leads us to the righteousness that comes from the Cross. There, upon overthrown human greatness, rests God's glory. There, where dead creation crucified the living God. There, where people erected a tower to the heavens but could not reach Him, God became a man. There, where the king intended to build a palace to the Creator, in return, He made us His temple. There, where God took curses instead of blessings, the instrument of His death became the road to our salvation.

## SEEKING GOD TAKES TIME

For three years, the Star Boy wandered the roads in search of his mother. Our journey will also be long, one not lined with ice cream cones or trays of sweets. Moses walked forty years in the wilderness. For ten years, Elisha followed Elijah. Jacob worked for fourteen years as a shepherd for Laban and only then received the promised Rachel.

Do not think that God will rush to you with open arms if you decide to devote yourself to knowing Him. At times, you will feel not like a welcome guest, but rather like a monk who spends three days in the rain seeking entrance to a monastery. This is not because God does not accept your desire. He will test, discipline, and educate you. Like Paul, you will begin to understand that you are not the least of the apostles but the chief among sinners; and instead of a heart, you have a tin can.

Habakkuk tells us how to travel down the difficult road before us:

> Though the fig tree does not bud
> and there are no grapes on the vines,
> though the olive crop fails
> and the fields produce no food,
> though there are no sheep in the pen
> and no cattle in the stalls,
> yet I will rejoice in the LORD,
> I will be joyful in God my Savior."[90]

On that journey, you will pass the way of Asaph as well:

> I thought about the former days,
> the years of long ago;
> I remembered my songs in the night.
> My heart meditated and my spirit asked:
> "Will the Lord reject forever?
> Will he never show his favor again?
> Has his unfailing love vanished forever?
> Has his promise failed for all time?
> Has God forgotten to be merciful?
> Has he in anger withheld his compassion?"
> Then I thought, "To this I will appeal:
> the years when the Most High stretched out his right hand."[91]

And this is only the beginning. We will have eternity in front of us to understand the One Who has no beginning, no end, no time limits, no creator, no master. The One Who gave everything and does not need anything in return; Who teaches everyone but Whom no one can teach; Who offers love instead of hate, forgiveness instead of revenge, and home instead of alien shelter. The One Who breathes life into us. The One Who calls us on the Way, but at the same time is both the Path and the Destination.

---

91   Psalm 77:5-10

# CHAPTER 7

# SALES ARE EVERYTHING

IN *THE PURSUIT OF GOD*, Aiden Tozer wrote:

> Every age has its own characteristics. Right now, we are in an
> age of religious complexity. The simplicity which is in Christ
> is rarely found among us. In its stead are programs, methods,
> organizations and a world of nervous activities which occupy
> time and attention but can never satisfy the longing of the heart.
> The shallowness of our inner experience, the hollowness of our
> worship, and that servile imitation of the world which marks
> our promotional methods all testify that we, in this day, know
> God only imperfectly, and the peace of God scarcely at all.[92]

When we in the mission were looking for the best form for the church,
I was annoyed. Why didn't Jesus in the Gospels or Paul in the book of Acts
give us the biblical form for the church? Then we would not have to rack our
brains. It could easily be written to do this or do that. Later, I realized that the
significance is not at all in the form but rather in the essence of what God
wants to convey to us.

It is very hard to capture that essence, though we have Scripture. In
ancient times, Christians sought out Anthony the Great to learn contemplation,
reflection, patience, forgiveness, and the search for Him from Whom come
the words of eternal life. Today we are ready to travel the world, to attend
conferences and seminars in search of the latest method or strategy. Ministers
seek God, requesting His help and blessings for their ministry; and when this

---

92   A.W. Tozer, ibid.

happens, they forget about Him and talk about their "method." It's as if Joshua left God, traveled to nearby regions, and conducted seminars on the "Seven Principles of City Destruction."[93] We teach others our "method," and when these "methods" do not work, our followers start looking for other teachers.

Paul wrote thirteen epistles, and he doesn't teach his disciples any methods or tools in any of them. Of course, one can draw methods out of his words, but I do not think that was his purpose; he was merely sharing his experience. Rather, he kneels before the Father "so that Christ may dwell in your hearts through faith. And I pray that you, being rooted and established in love, may have power, together with all the Lord's holy people, to grasp how wide and long and high and deep is the love of Christ, and to know this love that surpasses knowledge—that you may be filled to the measure of all the fullness of God."[94]

At a church planting seminar, during a break, the speaker asked me, "What do you think is the most effective method of evangelism?"

I replied, "The most effective method of evangelism is to evangelize." I think he did not expect a response like that.

Do not sign up for your third seminar on evangelism or read your fifth book on evangelism. Do not teach other people to preach the Gospel. Do not pray that God will send other people to evangelize. Just preach the Gospel. Approach a person; talk about your faith. It's really quite simple. However, it is not so easy to actually do it.

What will help? Knowing God and . . . well, that alone is the answer to every question.

In business, there is an expression: "Sales are Everything." If a company has the best marketers, an outstanding strategy, an office on a prestigious street, but no sales, then the business is finished.

So, here it is: Knowing God is everything.

---

93   See Joshua 6.
94   Ephesians 3:17-19

**Question**: Do you want to be a good husband?
**Answer**: Know God.

**Question**: Do you want to become a businessman after the heart of God?
**Answer**: Know God.

**Question**: Do you want to know why you came to this world?
**Answer**: Know God.

**Question**: I am a missionary. What do I do if I have no desire to share the Gospel?
**Answer**: Know God.

Regarding evangelism, I'm not saying that by developing your relationship with God, you will completely forget fear or that you will always know what to say. You still need to be proactive. But there is a difference between duty and initiative.

| Duty | Initiative |
|---|---|
| "In my opinion, I do not fully believe all that. How can I talk about something that I have not experienced myself? Are people really doomed to eternal suffering? In my opinion, they are doing just fine as they are. Today, the pastor preached a lot from the Scripture; in my opinion, not everything in the Bible is reliable. Yet, I still need to tell people about God because that is the duty of every church member. | "It's great to be a believer. Every day, I learn more about God, how much He loves me, and I didn't even think that I was such a sinner. The man sitting next to me does not yet know the living God. But I'm a little scared to talk to him. What if he doesn't want to listen to me? God, help me so that I can step out and share the most valuable thing I have. |

Successful evangelism does not begin with evangelism; it begins with God.

Let's do a thought experiment. Consider two believers, each wanting to become a husband and father after the heart of God. The first will spend two years reading books, attending seminars and group discussions on the topic of family. However, he will have little time with God; he won't seek God. The second believer will do nothing like that. He will devote himself only to knowing God, spending much time in contemplation, in prayer, and in meditation on the Word; he will learn to hear the voice of God and obey Him. If he reads books, then they are on the topic of knowing God. At the end of two years, who do you think will be the better father, the better husband? Applying methods without knowing God is like trying to plant flowers on the deck of a steel ship.

Do you want to affect the world for God? Do you want to be a messenger, not a tourist? Devote two years to knowing God. (Of course, it's necessary to devote your entire life to this, but it's *really* necessary to start somewhere.)

Don't live under this delusion: If I go to church, read the Bible, and work in full-time ministry, then I automatically know God. There is a difference between going to church and knowing God, between being married and having a relationship with your spouse, between working for the government and serving your country. In order to know God, you need not give up everything and withdraw to the desert (for there is enough desert in the modern world). I understand that no mission would support such a missionary. Continue in your ministry, whether it be founding a church, teaching in a seminary, or translating the Bible into a local language. But in all that you do—during your quiet time, while meditating on Scripture, in planting a church, when spending time with family, through evangelizing, when reading Christian literature, or by communicating with friends—in all this, seek God above all else.

The U.S.S.R. national hockey team under Anatoly Tarasov was the champion in all international competitions for nine consecutive years from 1963 to 1971. This legendary coach taught his athletes to devote themselves to hockey. One day, he saw one of the players clearing the area of snow.

He asked, "What are you doing?"

"What do you mean? I'm shoveling snow."

Tarasov replied, "Don't just shovel snow; work on your slapshot."

So, what does God want to teach my children? How does God look at our church? How can I be a light to my neighbors?

This means changing your mirror into a window. In a mirror, you see only yourself; through a window, you learn to see Him. When this happens, He will produce the greatest miracle of your life—not walking on water, and not feeding five thousand, and not turning water into wine. The greatest miracle is a change in the human heart, when the fossils of your heart turn into tulips. For true service comes from the heart.

There may come a time when we gather for a conference in Jakarta—where Navigators, Campus Crusade, Pioneers, Southern Baptists, and local believers assemble not to discuss church planting, Sunday School programs, or new media technologies, but to share the experience of knowing Him of Whom John Calvin wrote:

> But although our mind cannot conceive of God, without rendering some worship to him, it will not, however, be sufficient simply to hold that he is the only being whom all ought to worship and adore, unless we are also persuaded that he is the fountain of all goodness, and that we must seek everything in him, and in none but him. My meaning is: we must be persuaded not only that as he once formed the world, so he sustains it by his boundless power, governs it by his wisdom, preserves it by his goodness, in particular, rules the human race with justice and Judgment, bears with them in mercy, shields them by his protection; but also that not a particle of light, or wisdom, or justice, or power, or rectitude, or genuine truth, will anywhere be found, which does not flow from him, and of which he is not the cause; in this way we must learn to expect and ask all things from him, and thankfully ascribe to him whatever we receive.[95]

---

95   Calvin, ibid.

# CHAPTER 8

# UNDER THE RULE OF "GODS"

## THE WONDERS OF STATISTICS AND THE POWER OF BUDGET

IT IS NOT BY CHANCE that I provide an entire chapter for such an important topic. How could I not? For in our mission, statistics seemed to be the fourth person in the Trinity. We created statistics on each seminar held, on each church meeting, on each step, and on every breath. The bigger the numbers were, the more efficiently this god worked in our region. Indeed, we ruled this god.

As I said before, we were looking for partners among the large, established, traditional churches in Central Asia. A church of one hundred people in a Muslim region is the same as a church of three thousand in Colorado. We offered our vision; and if they agreed, then we held a seminar on the "latest" methods of church planting. We taught the cell model of Ralph Neighbor, the movement of the house churches of David Garrison, the organic church of Neil Cole. I am not against these strategies—each of them has its own strengths, and each can be effective in a specific context. I am against using these methods as a "magic tool," and I am against being taught by people who have no experience with it themselves or who did not achieve a lasting result.

These local churches had reason to join us—there was a big, Western mission behind us. We could financially support pastors, help with Bible education, and buy a car for the ministry. Things that the churches needed.

What did we need? We needed a movement. This is what everyone craved. You heard this buzzword in India, Uzbekistan, Russia, and the USA. But this movement did not occur here in Central Asia as it did in India—at least, not in the way they told us.

It is important to note here that behind our god—Statistics—there was an even more powerful god: Budget. If Moloch ate children, then Budget ate Statistics: the more gifts we gave to him, the more generous he was. So, we needed statistics, handed over every month, to attest to our movement. Therefore, we needed partners.

How did this work? Say, the pastor of a large, traditional church, inspired by a new technique that promised rapid growth, divided the church into cells and appointed a leader over each cell, which then began to function as a mini-church. There was a sermon, worship, communion, baptism, and even collected donations. Now, one could write that ten churches were founded. This is how the statistics worked. If by the end of the year, five cells had died and in the following year, another two, no one worried about that. Statistics handed over; money spent. This is how a movement was created.

In 2008, I studied at the Haggai Institute on the island of Maui, Hawaii, which brought together Christian leaders from third-world countries to learn leadership skills. One Sunday, on the bus to church, while sitting next to another student, I asked, "What country are you from?"

He replied, "Indonesia."

I was immediately interested. Indonesia was one of the most successful regions in the development of the home group movement. I asked, "How is the Gospel progressing in Indonesia? At a seminar, we were told that every fourth person in Indonesia is a believer."

He laughed for a long time until tears rolled down his cheeks. Then he said, "I heard about this statistic. Brother, I invite you to Indonesia."

Some churches miraculously survived; some became seriously ill but were able to survive the adaptation period; others had to start over. But there were few such churches. Many died. Therefore, every year, we were looking for more and more partners. This god demanded fresh sacrifices.

Over time, I began to realize that all this did not resemble the truth—what was happening in reality as opposed to what was typed in Excel. This was reminiscent of the Soviet era, when heads of collective farms and factories—in order not to lose bonuses or go to a correctional camp—turned huts into thriving farms and two sheep into a herd of horses—on paper, of course.

Therefore, in my reports, instead of "churches," I began to write "cells" or "home groups," and I explained that they were part of an existing church about which we had reported the previous year. However, when we received the next quarterly newsletter reporting on the activities of our mission, there were no home groups mentioned; in Texas, they had been turned into churches.

Then we local ministers talked among ourselves about the need to change our existing strategy. What we had been trying to implement had not been verified to actually work. It did not help churches but, on the contrary, brought harm. We said, "Let's try it ourselves; we will get a good result and, only after that, will we teach others."

At first, the home office didn't listen to us. But then, at the next reporting conference, we were able to talk with our field director, Brent. He listened carefully and said, "Good. Do it."

This is what we needed, but I had spent many years in the mission, so I knew how it worked. I told him, "You should know that our statistics will drop."

He answered, "We are moved by God, not by statistics."

For the first time, we focused our strength on our own ministry. We started churches, cells, and home groups on our own. We continued to work with partners, but this was secondary to the main work.

In the first year, statistics fell by seventy percent. A year later, our budget was cut by forty percent, and a year after that, by another twenty percent. At the same time, ministers resigned or were fired. By the time I left the mission, the budget was fifteen to twenty percent of what it had been, and staff had decreased by seventy percent.

After that, tell me that statistics do not matter. It seems that god, having ceased to receive gifts, became angry. He turned out to have more power than our field director, who was transferred to another region a couple of years later. Great is the wrath of this god.

However, when we read the New Testament, we see that the sovereign god Budget, who has learned so well how to manage missions, does not have authority over Jesus:

> They went across the lake to the region of the Gerasenes. When Jesus got out of the boat, a man with an evil spirit came from the tombs to meet him. This man lived in the tombs, and no one could bind him anymore, not even with a chain. For he had often been chained hand and foot, but he tore the chains apart and broke the irons on his feet. No one was strong enough to subdue him. Night and day among the tombs and in the hills he would cry out and cut himself with stones. When he saw Jesus from a distance, he ran and fell on his knees in front of him.
>
> He shouted at the top of his voice, "What do you want with me, Jesus, Son of the Most High God? In God's name don't torture me!" For Jesus had said to him, "Come out of this man, you impure spirit!"
>
> Then Jesus asked him, "What is your name?"
>
> "My name is Legion," he replied, "for we are many." And he begged Jesus again and again not to send them out of the area.
>
> A large herd of pigs was feeding on the nearby hillside. The demons begged Jesus, "Send us among the pigs; allow us to go into them." He gave them permission, and the impure spirits came out and went into the pigs. The herd, about two thousand in number, rushed down the steep bank into the lake and were drowned.
>
> Those tending the pigs ran off and reported this in the town and countryside, and the people went out to see what had happened.

When they came to Jesus, they saw the man who had been possessed by the legion of demons, sitting there, dressed and in his right mind; and they were afraid. Those who had seen it told the people what had happened to the demon-possessed man—and told about the pigs as well. Then the people began to plead with Jesus to leave their region.[96]

As a child, I traveled to the village during summer holidays. I liked many things there—a small river, the endless steppe, wild currant growing nearby, the passing train. But there was one thing I hated: Once a week, my brother and I had to get up at 4:30 in the morning to herd the sheep, and not only our sheep but all our neighbors' sheep as well. All the villagers herded the sheep in turns.

Therefore, I understand why the Gerasenes asked Jesus to leave, despite the fact that they witnessed such a miracle—these were their pigs. On their commodity exchange, the price of a pig was quoted above the price of a human life.

Not by chance, Mark, unlike Matthew, indicates the number of pigs as being "about two thousand." Let's do the math. If we figure the cost of one pig as three hundred dollars in today's dollars, then the value of the dead pigs was six hundred thousand dollars. It turns out, to save one person, Jesus spent more than half a million dollars. If Jesus worked in our mission with such statistics and with such a flippant attitude toward the budget, He would have been fired long ago.

Money had no power over Jesus. However, it has often happened that money has power over His disciples, both ancient and contemporary.

While he was in Bethany, reclining at the table in the home of a man known as Simon the Leper, a woman came with an alabaster jar of very expensive perfume, made of pure nard. She broke the jar and poured the perfume on his head.

> Some of those present were saying indignantly to one another, "Why this waste of perfume? It could have been sold for more than a year's wages and the money given to the poor." And they rebuked her harshly.
>
> "Leave her alone," said Jesus. "Why are you bothering her? She has done a beautiful thing to me. The poor you will always have with you, and you can help them any time you want. But you will not always have me. She did what she could. She poured perfume on my body beforehand to prepare for my burial. Truly I tell you, wherever the gospel is preached throughout the world, what she has done will also be told, in memory of her."[97]

Some disciples pounced on the woman, "Why this waste of perfume?" Which really means, "Why are you abusing the budget?" And again, Mark, not by chance and in contrast to Matthew, gives the value of the perfume as being three hundred denarii, a year's wages.[98]

A woman enters. We do not know who she is or where she is from, but she sees Christ before her. The disciples see three hundred denarii.

In this chapter, I do not mean to say that money doesn't matter. Scripture says, "Money is the answer for everything."[99] I know that we need to be "wise stewards." I surely know how hard it is to raise support and identify donors. But I have a question: Who are we following?

Imagine this situation: Missionary Bruce is the head of a mission organization in Ukraine. The mission began work in the early nineties when it was possible to rent an apartment for fifty dollars a month or buy a building for the church for ten thousand dollars; the cost of one meal was less than a dollar. Twenty years later, the cost of living in Ukraine has risen by ten times, but the mission budget has remained the same. Bruce does not know what to do. One night, he goes to bed, and Jesus appears to him in a dream.

---

97   Mark 14:3-9
98   See Matthew 20.
99   Ecclesiastes 10:19b

Jesus says, "Bruce, prices in Ukraine have risen; therefore, close the ministry in Ukraine and transfer it to Africa. It's cheaper there. If in ten years, prices there also rise, I will then speak to you where next to move the ministry. Wait for the next dream."

In the morning, Bruce wakes up and falls on his knees. "Thank You, God, for this great revelation. We had no idea what to do."

Our field director, Brent, regretted that the cost of one seminar in Kazakhstan would pay for ten seminars in India. Are we following God's voice or budget, statistics, and logic?

God can call your church to send missionaries to Russia, and you can then send them to Mexico because it is closer and cheaper (and it's not for nothing that we studied Spanish in school). Then we wonder, "Why does our 'wise' ministry go nowhere?!" I believe that if God calls someone to open a church in Tokyo, this should be done, despite the fact that it's the most expensive city in the world. As for money, Jesus can get it from the belly of a fish (see Matt. 17:27). Let Jesus create these churches instead of men creating Excel spreadsheets.

CHAPTER 9

# LOVE THY NEIGHBOR

*But he wanted to justify himself, so he asked Jesus, "And who is my neighbor?"*[100]

I REMEMBER HOW WE SAW Caleb off after he had served three years in our mission. On the ground floor, a table was set with pizza, cakes, and Coca-Cola. We said warm words, prayed, and sang along with a guitar. Even after I'd been ten years in the mission, missionaries simply shook my hand. I did not take offense because I knew that's the way foreigners said goodbye to any local minister. We said goodbye as if we were all agents of the CIA or the KGB: secretly, quietly, and preferably without any consequences. As in the movie *The Recruit*, "He will become a star on the wall, a blank on the page of the book."[101] But this is an epilogue. What was the preface?

In John Steinbeck's novel *The Grapes of Wrath*, the Joads, a family of farmers, leave their home in Oklahoma and, along with thousands of other families, go to sunny California. Dust storms, equipment failures, banks, corporations, and corporate agents forced them to leave the land of their fathers and go where they can eat "grapes and oranges as much as you please."[102]

In the same way, we locals in the 1990s and the beginning of the 2000s, left our jobs and went to work for foreign missions. Teachers, engineers, doctors, lawyers, firemen, sales representatives—all turned into full-time ministers.

---

100  Luke 10:29
101  *The Recruit*, Directed by Roger Donaldson, Burbank: Touchstone Pictures, 2003.
102  John Steinbeck, *The Grapes of Wrath* (New York City: Viking, 1939).

We came to the Light of Truth,[103] Campus Crusade, YWAM, Pioneers, German and Korean missions, and The Bible Society.

Steinbeck's heroes were looking for a better life, whereas we were looking for the will of God. At that time, the most popular message of the preachers was, "If you really want to follow God, become a *full-time* minister."

After graduating from the institute, my friend, a missionary named Charles, asked, "What do you want to be?"

I replied, "Either a businessman or a politician."

He looked at me as if I had said that I was going to put together a gang and rob trains. Then he said, "Well, we need politicians." *Businessman* was a swear word.

If a person wanted to be a businessman, manager, or official, people looked at him as though he loved the world. One of the most popular texts for conviction of this "sin" was the book of Jonah. A person who did not want to enter full time mission work with an organization or church was labeled a Jonah (though we later realized that's not what the book was about).

At that time, one would hear testimonies like, "I used to earn good money, building my career, working in business. Now I have nothing, but I serve in a mission." Other locals looked upon the ministers as if they were celestials.

The Joad family reached California and found a beautiful country and good land, but it also had sheriffs with nightsticks, low wages, and citizenship in Hooverville. We, on our mission, also did not expect what we saw.

All of us imagined the mission was a "holy" place—a place that knew of David Livingstone, William Carey, Pavel Pavlov, and George Müller. Here, people came to live and die for God. In reality, the mission looked like a "land of sinners."

In *The Grapes of Wrath*, the country was divided into two nations: masters and aliens. We were divided into missionaries and locals. It's like two rivers that flow parallel to each other: one wide, rich in fish, with green shores; the

---

103   The mission with which I worked, based in Dallas—the name has been changed in this book.

other narrow, shallow, with banks that had collapsed into the river. These rivers never intersect. If you look from afar, it may seem that they merge together, but this is an illusion, a mirage. We walked in the same hallways, read the same books, went to the same church. Even though we had one God, we lived on different planets.

In 2007, I became the Director of Christian Education for Turkic-speaking regions. In various Central Asian cities, we ran schools that taught the Word of God in the national language. In each school, I needed to appoint a representative who would be responsible for checking homework, working with teachers, and organizing the school. I sat in the administrative office and discussed the details of the ministry with a colleague.

My colleague asked, "What salary do you want to pay Timur?" (Timur was to become the representative of our ministry in one of the key cities of Uzbekistan.)

"One hundred dollars," I replied.

In the corner of the office, Karen, the financial director of our organization, was sitting at her computer. She remarked, "Isn't that a bit much?"

I wanted to turn to her and say, "Maybe you'll go there, and we'll pay you one hundred dollars!" Naturally, I did not say anything, for though I bore the grand title of director, I was but a local, and merely having my own opinion was enough to get me fired.

Let me show what one hundred dollars would buy in Kazakhstan at that time:

- Levi's Original Jeans,
- One month's rent for a one-room apartment, un-remodeled,
- One month of food for two people and the basic necessities,
- Economy class airplane flight from Almaty to Tashkent, or
- Nokia cell phone

Therefore, Timur's monthly salary was the price of a cell phone. Prices in Uzbekistan were about the same. Renting an apartment was cheaper; tea and sugar were more expensive.

When I set the salary of one hundred dollars, was I more generous or fair compared to my sister from America? No, I was not. I was just wearing the same shoes.

Often, local believers heard reproaches from Muslims: "You sold out to the Americans; you believe in Jesus because you are paid." I sold out so well that I did not have enough money for the bus. Since Almaty is in the mountains on a slope, and the apartment I rented was located above the mission building, I walked from the apartment to the mission and went back on the bus in order to save money. When I was sick, I couldn't go to the state doctor because I wasn't registered in the apartment I rented—landlords are unwilling to register anyone in their apartments—and there was no money for a private doctor. One of the teachers of the seminary was a former doctor, so I turned to him. He said that he could not diagnose me without tests (which I could not afford), but when I insisted, he sent me to the pharmacy for medicine. Sometimes, it helped, sometimes not. Singles could live in a dorm room with students. When our salary increased to two hundred dollars, we were told, "Since the salary is higher, you have to pay rent." They put in one pocket but took from another.

You may think that this chapter is about money: "Missionaries are bad; they paid such small salaries." But really, this chapter is about attitude.

In Steinbeck's *Grapes of Wrath*, we see the pain of people, and it is not related to the fact that some were rich while others lived in tents. It's related to the attitude of Californians. The migrants said, "Our families go back seven generations born and raised in America, and if we dig deeper, we find Irish, Scots, Germans, and British. One of our ancestors fought for the revolution, and many participated in the civil war, on both sides. We are Americans."[104] But residents of the Golden State gave them the insulting nickname "Okie" (abbreviated from Oklahoma) and treated them as strangers, aliens, barbarians.

---

104  Steinbeck, ibid.

We are told that we are one family; we are brothers and sisters! Really? Well, I began to think seriously after one incident.

Since our mission served throughout Central Asia, we often went on business trips and were given a per diem, a daily allowance. Because it was mission money, which means it belongs to God, we tried to save whenever we could. We tried not to use a taxi inside the city; we bought less and cheaper food. If there was any money remaining after the trip, we always returned it to our bookkeeper. One morning, I spoke with Elvira, our first local HR director. In the conversation, I remarked that I needed to go to the accounting department and return my per diem.

She asked, "What for?"

"I've always done it."

"By law, we give you a daily allowance. This is the amount set by law, and if you have something left, you don't need to return it."

"Have the laws changed?"

"They've always been like that."

Going down to the bookkeeper's office, I said to the accountant, "Elvira said that according to the law, I don't have to return my per diem."

"Well, then, don't return it."

"Why did we return it before?"

"You gave it by your own initiative."

"But why didn't you tell me that by law, I don't need to return the money?"

After the financial director, Karen, left the office, the accountant whispered, "I have nothing to do with it. The mission's leadership decided that you all should return the per diem."

Missionaries who lived in private homes in the best parts of town, had two cars, went to ski resorts in the winter, and took trips home to the USA (or if they couldn't afford that, took their families to Turkey or Egypt)—how could they decide that people who received two hundred dollars a month must return their per diem?

If you are a missionary, be careful about what you say and what you do. We locals do not yet know that for some of you, the words "brothers and sisters" are simply placeholder terms of the Christian subculture and that "I will pray for you" most often means "I cannot help you."

We asked for help with English language studies and were told, "We know an inexpensive course." But when we were asked on Saturday to show guests around the city, we didn't say, "We know an inexpensive travel agency." Why is it that way? Why, when a local says no, does he "lack the heart of a minister," yet when a missionary says no, he "knows how to set boundaries?"

Consider this passage:

> On one occasion an expert in the law stood up to test Jesus. "Teacher," he asked, "what must I do to inherit eternal life?"
>
> "What is written in the Law?" he replied. "How do you read it?"
>
> He answered: "'Love the Lord your God with all your heart and with all your soul and with all your strength and with all your mind'; and, 'Love your neighbor as yourself.'"
>
> "You have answered correctly," Jesus replied. "Do this and you will live."
>
> But he wanted to justify himself, so he asked Jesus, "And who is my neighbor?"
>
> In reply Jesus said: "A man was going down from Jerusalem to Jericho, when he was attacked by robbers. They stripped him of his clothes, beat him and went away, leaving him half dead. A priest happened to be going down the same road, and when he saw the man, he passed by on the other side. So too, a Levite, when he came to the place and saw him, passed by on the other side. But a Samaritan, as he traveled, came where the man was; and when he saw him, he took pity on him. He went to him and bandaged his wounds, pouring on oil and wine. Then he put the man on his own donkey, brought him to an inn and took care of him. The next day he took out two denarii and gave them to the innkeeper. 'Look after him,' he said, 'and when I return, I will reimburse you for any extra expense you may have.'

> "Which of these three do you think was a neighbor to the man
> who fell into the hands of robbers?"
> The expert in the law replied, "The one who had mercy on him."
> Jesus told him, "Go and do likewise."[105]

The lawyer comes to Jesus with a question, and Jesus, as usual, answers the question with a question. The lawyer gives an answer, and the Lord praises him. Not many people, including the disciples, could get a similar assessment. However, the lawyer asks another question, "And who is my neighbor?" This is the crucial question in the passage. It is not by accident that the lawyer asks this particular question.

The fact is that the phrase "love your neighbor as yourself" is taken from Leviticus chapter nineteen. We open the original source and see that this is the second part of the phrase, which reads in full, "Do not seek revenge or bear a grudge against anyone among your people, but love your neighbor as yourself. I am the LORD."[106]

If we use the historical-grammatical method and apply the Golden Rule—to let Scripture interpret Scripture—we see that the second part of the sentence follows logically from the first. Let's also look at the context of what comes before: "Do not go about spreading slander among your people. Do not do anything that endangers your neighbor's life. I am the LORD. Do not hate a fellow Israelite in your heart. Rebuke your neighbor frankly so you will not share in their guilt."[107]

Studying the passages, we come to one conclusion: the neighbor is an Israelite. When speaking with the lawyer, Jesus expands the boundaries of the Pentateuch.

If we additionally refer to Paul's letter to the Colossians, we see that the New Testament erases religious, national, cultural, and social boundaries: "Put on the new self, which is being renewed in knowledge in the image of

---

105  Luke 10:25-37
106  Leviticus 19:18
107  Leviticus 19:16-17

its Creator. Here there is no Greek or Jew, circumcised or uncircumcised, barbarian, Scythian, slave or free, but Christ is all, and is in all."[108]

But despite all this, the question "Who is my neighbor?" remains relevant to this day. Theologically, love has no limits. Practically, the borders of love can be fenced with barbed wire and guarded by dogs.

Therefore, I cannot help asking you, how do you see us locals? As Samaritans? As inhabitants of a third world country?

True, I understand that many missionaries will not comprehend what I am saying, and those who do may not admit it.

At the seminary, the leadership course was taught by a visiting professor from the Dallas seminary. We had an interesting dialogue about national sins. We said that in earlier times in Kazakhstan, it was customary to kidnap "brides" against their will. The teacher said, "This is a sin you need to repent of." We said there were wars with other nations to expand our territory. The teacher said, "This is a sin you need to repent of." We said in our country corruption is everywhere. The teacher said, "This is a sin you need to repent of." Then we said, "And you know, bad things happened in America, too. America dropped the atomic bomb on Hiroshima and Nagasaki. White people oppressed black people—" Here, the teacher interrupted, "Oh, these are not sins. That's just politics."

Also, our missionaries had many different terms to describe sin. There was one "favorite" sin which they all recognized—sexual sin, like adultery or viewing pornography. They preached about it, condemned it, and could excommunicate you for it. However, if it was something else . . . If they did not keep their word, it meant that they had a change of vision. If they had double standards, it was a new strategy. If they were not hospitable, it was just American culture. Pride was leadership principles, and indifference was just a different perspective.

Western ministers have thousands of advantages over us: they are better educated than we are; they have more experience; they have big churches and a strong economy behind them; they founded Princeton University and Trinity

---

Evangelical Divinity School; they wrote *Mere Christianity* and *Pilgrim's Progress*; they learned from Charles Spurgeon and Jonathan Edwards. It makes no sense to list everything. We have only one thing: we know that we are sinners.

Do not listen to me; listen to the Scriptures: "So in everything, do to others what you would have them do to you, for this sums up the Law and the Prophets."[109] So, if you hire a local employee, treat him fair and square. You cannot hire a minister and give him support that's less than the cost of renting a one-room apartment and then pretend that you know nothing.

I am not saying that the financial support of a local minister should be equal to the support of a Western missionary; we are in different weight categories. The average salary in Canada and the average salary in Mongolia are incomparable. But please cover four basic needs: housing, food, clothing, and medicine. If something remains for a rainy day and to treat the kids to ice cream, it's great!

If you cannot offer that basic amount, then let them go to regular work where they can earn more and serve in their free time. This has many advantages. They will be able to provide for their family; they will not assume that someone owes them something. They will never ask, "With whom can I share the Gospel?"

If you've been a full-time minister for many years, you know what I mean. Over time, a professional minister does not retain any contacts outside of his believing friends. So, he needs to create some artificial evangelical pools, like an English club, business meetings, or an outreach in the park.

But there is another important advantage. When I served in the mission, my parishioners told me, "You can _____ (fill in the blank: preach the Gospel, practice discipleship, serve, etc.) because that's your job and you're paid for to do it. We work in a normal job, and we don't have time for all that. It's impossible."

For the past seven years, I have worked just like everyone else from nine a.m. to six p.m. I take two or three business trips per month. I have a wife and three children. I lead meetings, prepare sermons, teach leaders, visit brothers, and

109  Matthew 7:12

preach the Gospel—just like many other lay leaders around the world. During all this time, not a single church member has dared say, "I cannot preach the Gospel because I have a family," or "I cannot prepare a sermon because I have no time."

Therefore, let them earn their own bread. Flee from preachers who say, "The only true ministers are *full-time* ministers."

By the way, your true authority will manifest itself in this situation. It is easy to inspire when you pay a salary, but can you be an example to local leaders when you have no formal influence? And do not be like some who hire thirty people for the support of ten and then are proud that they have such a big mission.

I want to talk about one more thing. When we came to the mission, we understood that we dedicate ourselves not only to God but also to the mission. But was the mission ready to devote itself to us?

In Uzbekistan, persecution of the Church began at the end of 2005, under president Islam Karimov. Buildings were taken from churches; missionaries were deported; and some local leaders were jailed. During this time, my fellow student at seminary, Igor, pastor of a large church, came to a missionary who was hastily packing his suitcases. Igor told him that a minister from their mission had been arrested.

Igor asked, "Will you visit him in jail?"

"It's not possible. It's out of my hands. The embassy ordered all Americans to leave the country. I am a citizen of another state."

Igor went to the prison and told the minister that the mission had left the country. The man wept—not because he was put in prison but because the mission for which he had worked so hard had abandoned him.

In case anything goes wrong, you can return to your homeland, but where can we go? I know that nowadays Oklahomans and Texans have become Californians, yet we locals have become Okies. But Okies are human beings, too.

Therefore, before winning the world, win the heart of the one who is beside you.

CHAPTER 10

# THE MISSION OF JOHN THE BAPTIST

*They came to John and said to him, "Rabbi, that man who was with you on the*
*other side of the Jordan—the one you testified about—look, he is baptizing,*
*and everyone is going to him."[110]*

*He must become greater; I must become less.[111]*

SEVERAL JEWS SAT ON THE bank of the river. The sun burned their heads;
sweat seeped through their robes. They were thinking, *Well, we can skip*
*rocks as long as we don't spray the teacher. We can take another swim.* There was
absolutely nothing to do.

Suddenly, they saw two men walking toward them, arguing: "Azariah, I'm
telling you, let's get out of here."

One of the Jews ran to the men and said, "Come with us, the teacher will
baptize you. We will tell you what to do."

"Azariah, I'll say it again, no one comes here anymore. All Israel is following Jesus."

"Come, we do it differently now; we have more water. It is very convenient."

"Azaria, it's once in a lifetime; everyone will laugh at us."

"Okay, Zalman, we'll do what you want. I hope we won't regret it. Let's
go to Jesus."

Seeing the retreating figures, the hearts of the disciples were filled with
pain. The Pharisees were right: everyone was following Jesus.

---

110  John 3:26
111  John 3:30

Approaching John, the most courageous disciple said, "Teacher, the One Who was with you at the Jordan and about Whom you testified is baptizing, and everyone goes to Him. Why don't you tell Him to stop?"

Other disciples joined in. "That's right. And why did you tell everyone about Him? Stop Him. Tell Him it's your business. You were sent by God to do this. Why is He taking it away from you?"

The disciples were pained for their teacher; he had been through so many trials and hardships. He had next to nothing, and now what little he had was being taken away.

John's mission is the key that opens the door for the true ministry of a missionary. What was the mission of John the Baptist?

"Finally they said, 'Who are you? Give us an answer to take back to those who sent us. What do you say about yourself?' John replied in the words of Isaiah the prophet, 'I am the voice of one calling in the wilderness, *Make straight the way for the Lord.*'"[112] He told his disciples, "He is the one who comes after me, the straps of whose sandals I am not worthy to untie."[113]

Just as John came to prepare the way for the Lord, missionaries must prepare the way for local leaders.

## SUN AND MOON

Frank, the head of evangelism of our mission, whose headquarters were in Dallas, wrote me a letter as the Director of Church Development in Central Asia. He reported that they had money to buy a good and expensive photocopier for one of our key partners, a church in Kyrgyzstan, which was actively involved in evangelism. After reading the letter, I immediately contacted the pastor of the church.

It turned out that they did not need a copy machine to print evangelistic literature. First, the cost of printing at private copy centers was so small that owning a photocopier did not make it less expensive; and second, the

112   John 1:22-23
113   John 3:27

presence of a copy machine could be used against the church in the future as evidence of the spread of illegal religious literature.

However, they had another idea for using the money. Every month, a team of five or six people, having loaded their car with literature, would travel to remote areas for evangelism. Their car was old and often broke down, so they asked if they could use the money to buy a new car or overhaul the old one.

I wrote a letter to Frank and received his reply: "Kanat, this is a great idea, but I think that having their own copy machine will significantly improve evangelism in the region. They'll be able to print whatever literature they want." I wrote another letter to Frank explaining in detail the pastor's arguments, just the same as in my previous letter. He wrote me another letter with a similar answer. After we both wrote a total of seven letters, I just stopped writing.

What is the radical difference between the ministry of John the Baptist and the ministry of foreign missions? John did not have an independent ministry. He helped prepare for the ministry of Jesus. His ministry was secondary, supportive. His ministry had no meaning without the ministry of Christ. It's like having a reception desk without a hotel, a boarding gate without a plane.

The disciples of John were pained for the ministry of their teacher, only because they did not see the full picture. If you look at the ministry of John in Aenon as an independent ministry, then it was a complete failure. But if you look at the ministry of John and the ministry of Jesus as a single ministry, then it was a great victory. The victory of John the Baptist.

The modern ministry of foreign missions is an attempt by modern-day John the Baptists to become Christ. The motto of John the Baptist: "He must increase, and I must decrease." The motto of the foreign mission: "Do what we say, or we don't need you."

Jesus said that "the people of this world are more shrewd in dealing with their own kind than are the people of the light."[114] A revolution occurred in business that has not yet occurred in ministry. There have been two eras in business: the era of Sales and the era of Marketing. In the era of Sales, the primary focus was on the product. The approach was as follows: I have a product; I suggest that you buy it from me. If it does not suit you, this is your problem; I have nothing else. The era of Marketing creates a product based on a customer's need.

In business, the focus has shifted from products, concepts, and development to the customer's need. Similarly, the focus of Western missionary organizations must shift from the missions themselves to the needs of local leaders. "I am not the Messiah but am sent ahead of him."[115] Today, locals are considered to be merely a work force helping the mission implement *their* plans and projects. The key word in that sentence is *their*. In eighteen years of service, I don't remember a missionary coming up and asking, "Kanat, how can I help your ministry?" Mostly, they just told me what to do, what to pray for, and when to show up.

Many missions hire local ministers, convey the vision of their mission, tell them what to do, and then call it "development of local leadership." True development of local leaders is when you come to a person who is not from your mission, not from your denomination, not from your church, and asking, "How can we help you realize your God-given call?" Ask this question not just to get a checkmark on your paper but to do everything possible to help realize the leader's potential.

This is difficult to do. Nobody wants to be a boy who brings a glass of water; everyone wants to stand in the pulpit and preach. This is the heavy burden of John the Baptist.

So, in the conversation with Frank about the photocopier, I wondered why he would not give the church what they needed, and he wondered why I didn't do what he was telling me to do.

This change of perspective should concern not only individual missionaries but also mission leadership because a smart soldier does not

---

115  John 3:28b

give orders to the army. Also, it is difficult for "low ranking" missionaries to change the system inclusive of field directors, presidents, and boards of missionary organizations. I was surprised by the ability of some executives in our mission to create ingenious strategies for Turkmenistan, Uzbekistan, and Kazakhstan without leaving their office in Dallas. I imagine some could not have found Turkmenistan on the globe.

I appeal to mission leaders: Please listen to your soldiers on the battlefield. Believe me, a person who has faithfully served in Mozambique for ten years knows the culture, mentality, and needs of the people better than you, despite the fact that he doesn't have the title of vice president, did not graduate from George Washington University, and did not write a book on missions. Do not follow the principle, "There are only two opinions: my way or the wrong way."

There is yet another reason why missions need to focus on training local leaders, and every year it becomes more relevant. One of the largest diasporas in Central Asia is Koreans. Based on the decree of the Council of People's Commissars and the Central Committee of the CPSU (b) No. 1428-326 "On the Eviction of the Korean Population from the Border Areas of the Far Eastern Territory" signed by Stalin and Molotov, 172,000 ethnic Koreans were evicted from the borderlands of the Far East and relocated to uninhabited desert and empty lands in Kazakhstan and throughout Central Asia.[116] This is how Koreans appeared in Uzbekistan, Kazakhstan, Kyrgyzstan, and other parts of Central Asia.

After the collapse of the Soviet Union, missionaries from South Korea began to open missions and churches throughout Central Asia to reach these Koreans with the Gospel. Even though Koreans are not Westerners, locals see them as a part of Western missions because they come from a first world country and use almost exactly the same methods and approaches.

---

116 Wikipedia, "Deportation of Koreans in the USSR," Last modified September 2, 2020, https://en.wikipedia.org/wiki/Deportation_of_Koreans_in_the_Soviet_Union#:~:text=From%20September%20to%20October%201937,policy%20of%20systematic%20population%20transfer.

At the start of the nineties, the largest Korean diaspora was in Uzbekistan. Here, Korean missionaries opened churches, Bible schools, and cultural centers, where they taught Korean and Taekwondo. After twenty years of relative calm, persecution began in Uzbekistan. One of the consequences was the complete deportation of foreign religious workers. Within a month, every missionary had to leave the country.

Korean pastors came to the local leaders and said, "Take our church. We will leave you everything—the building, the apartment, our congregation." And local leaders said, "Why are you coming to us now? When you first arrived in Uzbekistan, we came to you and said, 'Let's serve together; together, we can do a lot.' But you said no."

In many countries, especially in the 10/40 window, religious laws are becoming tougher. Ten years ago in Central Asia, a missionary could officially be a pastor; today, it is difficult to get a visa. Fifteen years ago, missionaries could openly teach in seminaries; today, they are excluded from local church leadership.

Therefore, it is necessary to combine efforts. If we can do it in our generation, the result will exceed all expectations, where one plus one does not equal two but rather one hundred or one thousand. This is God's math. But so far, it hasn't been happening.

Today, communication between missionaries and local leaders is a conversation between the deaf and the dumb. We do not know what they are doing; they do not know what we are doing. We meet at weddings and garage sales. We are like the moon and the sun. At night, we see the moon, in the afternoon, the sun. They do not meet with each other. Yet if it does happen, it's considered a miracle.

As John said, "He must increase, but I must decrease." Your job is to help local leaders take their place and not think about how locals can serve your ministry. Let us all forget about the glory of Hudson Taylor and who will get the credit for the statistics—the Western mission or the local church—and let us together seek the glory of God.

At the end of the year, Karen approached and asked, "Kanat, when will you report for the money received for the copier?"

"What money?" I asked.

"Frank sent you money. He said you asked for money for a photocopier."

"I didn't ask him for money for a copy machine. I told him that we need money for a car for evangelism, but he didn't give his permission."

"Okay. I'll just say that you didn't use the money."

## CAN ANYTHING GOOD COME FROM NAZARETH?

In one of my training sessions, I conducted an experiment: I took out two poems and said that one poem was written by the Nobel laureate Joseph Brodsky and the other by Masha Smirnova, a first-year student in the literature department. Then I read both poems. Afterward, I asked, "Which poem did you like better?" Most students immediately praised the Nobel laureate's poem. After all the exclamations in favor of the great poet, I said that I cheated and that both poems were written by Joseph Brodsky. You should have seen their faces.

In elementary school, I wasn't a very good student. As I got older, I decided to improve my grades; but no matter how hard I tried, nothing worked. The teachers had their opinion of me; and no matter what I did, they saw me as a bad student. When I entered the Film Institute, nobody knew about my past. Therefore, from the start, I was getting straight A's. In the third year, I did not even need to take exams because the teacher would look at my previous grades and just write an A.

Walking through St. Petersburg, Russia, I could point out a man in an old, worn suit with an unkempt beard. Here is a little information about him: fifty-two years old, unmarried, does not communicate with anyone, does not have a job, lives with his mother, and both live on her pension. What would you think of him? What if I said that this is a very great mathematician, the only person who solved one of the Seven Millennium

Prize Problems, the Poincaré conjecture. His name is Grigori Perelman. It is not only the man and his appearance that matters but also what sort of opinion we have of him.

How do missionaries view local ministers? You can look at us as John the Baptist looked at Jesus: "Look, the Lamb of God, who takes away the sin of the world."[117] Or as Nathanael looked at Christ: "Nazareth! Can anything good come from there?"[118]

I was always taken aback by the surprise of some teachers who came from the Dallas Theological Seminary, the Southwest Baptist Seminary, the Trinity Bible School, or pastors and teachers of major churches in Texas, Oklahoma, Minnesota, Canada, and Australia. They were surprised that we could speak English; we read Donald Carson and asked difficult questions about topics from theological books we had read. So, I wondered if we should provide a short introduction at the airport, something like, "We do not live in caves and do not scratch an X instead of a signature."

If a local wants to be a leader in our mission, he has a long path ahead of him. It took me a total of six years to become the Regional Director of Christian Education, including three years as an assistant teacher, three years as a teacher serving in the mission, five years as the leader of a cell group, and three years as a preacher in the general assembly—all this in service in the church. Most Americans received leadership positions without having descended from the plane. Some immediately after seminary.

This happened not only inside the mission, but also in the churches. Once, my friend, the pastor of our church, approached me as an elder: "Kanat, Greg wants to serve in our church; we need to make him an elder."

Ivan, another elder, and I were indignant. "Why should we make him an elder? He hasn't served a single day in our church."

The pastor insisted, "But he is one of the leaders of our mission. He is . . ."

---

117  John 1:29b
118  John 1:46

"American?" I added, "I'll go to America. Do you think Willow Creek Church will make me an elder because I am Kazakh?"

Ali was the dean of our seminary. He was the best teacher of Old Testament and systematic theology in the Kazakh division; he graduated with honors from the Dallas Theological Seminary. He was also a fruitful pastor who founded two churches. Many leaders and pastors of our mission were from his first church and were his disciples. He served many years in our mission. When CATS turned into a real seminary, it needed a director, and the mission leadership started looking for one in the USA. Several local leaders appealed to the leadership for Ali to be appointed as the director. In actuality, he already was. He worked on the schedule, corresponded with teachers, engaged in organizing sessions, recruited students, and graded homework. And most importantly, no one loved the seminary more than he.

Our requests were met by silence. One of the vice presidents of the mission in Texas assumed responsibility as the head of our seminary. Ali continued to develop the seminary. A year later, a missionary came to us and was appointed director. He was a good, dedicated, open person, but if compared with Ali—from the point of view of understanding how the seminary worked, how to work with teachers and students, teaching skills, and experience in church ministry—the difference was like a kid who is learning to play basketball versus Kobe Bryant. But our "Kobe Bryant" had one big drawback—he was not American.

Why did that happen? This is due to how the Americans looked at the Americans and how the Americans looked at the Kazakhs. If you do not believe me and you are a missionary in Kazakhstan, Kenya, Puerto Rico, Mongolia, or Sri Lanka, do this: Ask local ministers (not your "favorites" and not those you pay), "Do you feel that we (Americans, Australians, Germans) look down upon you, that we treat our people one way and local people another, that we don't have a high opinion of you?"

I know that many missionaries will not ask this question because they are afraid of the answer. But there will be those who ask this question, though they don't need to, because they have a good connection with locals and will get a good, honest response. It's like the way we wonder why thin people run.

All that said, I don't mean that every missionary is like that. Was it an accident when Mark came and told me about the possibility of studying at the Phoenix Seminary? No. He saw something in me. He believed that I had potential. He saw a thirst for knowledge. But Mark is an odd believer. Once, he told me that every day, he and his wife ask each other, "How did I look like Christ today?" I don't know anyone who would do that, not among the "great" theologians, not among the gifted evangelists. However, Mark's problem was that even though he had enormous influence on local believers, he had no influence on other Americans.

When Nathanael said to Philip: "Can anything good come from Nazareth?," what was Philip's reply? "Come and see."[119]

Come and see us. Yes, we are from the third world countries. We did not invent the iPhone, and our countries do not occupy the first places in the Olympic Games. We do not have 286 Nobel laureates, and we do not have the best roads in the world.

But there are some things we can do. We can be sincere; we can keep our word; and we can follow Christ. When we say "brother" or "sister," we really mean it.

God has given gifts and talents not only to the inhabitants of foggy Albion, the New World, and the Basque Country, but also to the people of the land beyond the Indus River, the states of endless forests, and the countries of the great steppe.

The Kazakhs have a saying, "When Otrar was a city, London was a village." By the twelfth century, Otrar, an ancient city of Kazakhstan was a large trading center for handicrafts and art, with palaces, caravanserais, and city blocks. Otrar hosted one of the mints of the Karakhanid dynasty. It was the

---

119  John 1:46b

birthplace of many scholars, like the outstanding medieval mathematician and philosopher Al-Farabi, who authored commentaries on the writings of Aristotle and, therefore, received the honorary title "Second Teacher." Astronomer and mathematician Abbas Zhahari, along with Al-Khwarizmi, participated in the compilation of astronomical tables. The Otrar Library was considered the second largest after Alexandria.

For seventy years, Kazakhstan was part of the Soviet Union. The U.S.S.R. was the most literate country in the world. The U.S.S.R. launched the first man into space. The best chess players were found there. The best mathematical schools were located in the U.S.S.R., as well as the best ballet.

And what about modern Kazakhstan? One member of my cell group moved to Canada with his family. In Almaty, he worked as a specialist in a telecommunications company. Before he left, people who knew about the move said in one voice, "You will not find a good job there. You will wash the floors in McDonald's. Our education is not respected there." But he did not give up and made a list of one hundred telecommunications companies in Canada. Arriving in Canada, he went to the first interview. He had to throw out his list because they hired him. He worked hard and stayed late. His first paycheck was higher than expected. As a believer, he went to the accounting department and said, "You made a mistake. You paid me too much." They said to him, "That's right. You always work overtime." Colleagues approached him and said, "Calm down. Why are you trying so hard?" Six months later, he was made head of the department.

Another friend, one of the leaders of our church, went to study in the USA. His children attended an American school. The teacher saw how well his son solved math problems and advised him to transfer to a stronger school, but he said it was difficult to do, that he would need to score at least thirty points on the entrance exam. My friend's son scored seventy points. On the English exam, he scored higher than eighty percent of the applicants.

These are just two simple examples.

I will cite a few examples of people who are considered to be great Americans:

- Jerry Yang, the founder of Yahoo!, is Taiwanese and moved to California with his parents at the age of ten.
- Madeleine Albright, the first female Secretary of State, is a Jew from Czechoslovakia who received American citizenship at the age of twenty.
- Hakeem Olajuwon, two-time NBA champion, lived in Nigeria up to age fifteen and went to the United States to get an education.
- Sergey Brin, the founder of Google, is a Soviet Jew, born in Moscow and raised in the USA at the age of five.
- Khaled Hosseini, one of the most widely read writers in the world, was born in Kabul, Afghanistan, and came to the United States at the age of fifteen.
- Elon Musk, the founder of SpaceX and Tesla, was born in South Africa and moved to North America at the age of seventeen.
- Bay Yumin, architect and designer of the Pyramid of the Louvre and the John F. Kennedy Library, is Chinese, born in Guangzhou and emigrated to the United States at the age of eighteen.
- Jan Koum, the founder of WhatsApp, was born in Kiev, Ukraine, and moved with his mother to California at the age of sixteen.

So, citizens of China, India, Russia, Mongolia, Afghanistan, Ukraine, Kenya, Algeria, Morocco, Kazakhstan, Iran, Congo, Peru, Colombia, and Moldova have potential. And it's not necessary to move to the USA in order to realize this potential.

In November of 2014, our national football (soccer) team was scheduled to oppose the Turkish national team in a qualifying match for the European championship. The day before the match, I read an interview with the foreign coach of our team: "The Turkish team plays a completely different class of game, and we have nothing to put against them. They are better than us in everything, and we will surely lose. But we will do everything in our power."[120] This coach and his team had lost before even taking the field.

Why am I telling you all this? To condemn you? No. I want you to have some faith in us. Mission leaders proclaiming, "We will win the world for Christ!" lose the battle before even leaving their native shores. How do you look at your team? What do you think of the local ministers? Do you see them as future Luthers and Spurgeons? Or do you think, "Can anything good come from Kazakhstan?"

## FINDING NEW LUTHERS

Do not look for Luthers among those who will look into your eyes, always agree with you, and say, "Yes, sir" and "No, sir." Future Luthers may not be employees of your mission, may not know English, and may be difficult to get along with. They will tell you the truth to your face, and they will talk with you as equals. They will have a mission in life: to glorify God and spread His Kingdom in their country. By the way, their calling may not be big, but it will be pure and unselfish. The mission may be composing praise songs in the Tatar language, opening a seminary for the Buryats, building a business in order to support ten pastors, establishing a church in the Far East, or constructing an orphanage.

In addition to the mission, they will have dedication. These are those who not only dream and talk about vision, but who actually do it. Understand that for them it is not just ministry or work. These people will not have the attitude, "If it works, great; but if not, so be it." These people do not play games; they are at war. They are warriors; they fight for their country. Pull out your sword and stand shoulder to shoulder with them; they will be honored to fight with you. And even if you do not join them, they will fight alone.

---

120  "Bernd Storck: 'When Kazakhstan began to beat Latvia, I got scared . . . ,'" Sports. kz, December 12, 2015, https://www.sports.kz/news/bernd-shtork-kogda-kazahstan- nachal-vyiigryivat-u-latvii-ya-ispugalsya.

## IN SEARCH OF A LEGACY

People make the argument that the church in the United States is dying, and therefore, churches should stop doing missionary work and only focus on local ministry. On the other hand, perhaps the church in the USA is still alive *because* of missionary activity. In Europe, churches have ceased missionary activity and have not grown stronger as a result. Today, the Cathedral of St. Peter, which was the center for the beginning of the Reformation, is no longer a temple of God but a tourist attraction. Nowadays in Germany, the birthplace of Martin Luther and Philip Melanchthon, a church of three hundred people, is considered large.

You can live by the principle, "We have our life; you have your life" and lock the Gospel within the borders of your country. But the result may be that the glaciers of Alaska, the lakes of Minnesota, the fields of Texas, the beaches of California, and the swamps of Florida will become the shores of the dead sea.

We need help today because some nations have followed Christ for fourteen hundred years and some only thirty.

Proverbs 3:28 says, "Do not say to your neighbor, 'Come back tomorrow and I'll give it to you'—when you already have it with you." Why does Scripture scream for urgency? Tomorrow, it may no longer be necessary or tomorrow may be too late because tomorrow is always ahead of us. When you decide to come tomorrow, it will become today, which will have its own tomorrow. Tomorrow may take only one day to destroy even the greatest ministry. We need help yesterday.

I have a question for those who are already here. When you leave, what will happen? When Cru, YWAM, Pioneers, Operation Mobilization, the Salvation Army, Korean and German missions leave, what will you leave behind? I'll tell you: laid-off employees.

What will they do after you're gone? Some will leave the ministry; others will start over and try to find their own way (but many will be much older). Or what happens most often, they will join another mission, run in the opposite direction, and believe in a new vision and promote other strategies. They will find another mom; they will never be independent. Tigers living in captivity die in the jungle.

At the beginning of the twentieth century, a Russian businessman opened a fish processing factory in the Far North. He calculated everything correctly. He bought fish directly from fishermen in bulk. The factory was on the seashore, so he did not have to transport the fish very far. He found cheap labor—the local Khanty people. It seemed like a win-win situation, but the factory suffered losses. Fish were stolen. Workers did not work well. Local gangsters did anything they wanted; when bandits went to the factory, the workers just left and waited for them to go away. The businessman lived far away in the city with his family, so he was not at the factory. The local manager was more afraid of his relatives than the owner. After much consideration, he found a solution: to make the factory a joint-stock company. He gave every worker a small share; and since the Khanty worked as a community, each family had quite a few. Workers stopped stealing—why steal from yourself? They kept each other accountable so that workers would come on time and not leave early. When the gangsters arrived, they stood at the factory gates: Men had rifles, and women brandished harpoons. The Khanty began to think of the factory as their own.

Why not choose the path of the Russian businessman? Rather than us helping build your ministry, you will help us build our ministry. When you leave, then what will happen? These ministries will remain. Why? Because it was not your ministry but our ministry.

Then, when we stand on our feet—when the Buryats go to the Mongols, when the Moroccans go to the Senegalese, and when the Uzbeks got to the Turkmen—we will become the second generation of John the Baptists. What about the Kazakhs? We can go to the Russians, the Chinese, or the Turks because, by descent, we are Turks, but we look Chinese and speak Russian very well!

Have you ever wondered why in one hundred years, Western missions have not achieved greater success in Turkey? Perhaps they await the Kazakh missionaries. When I was in Istanbul and the Turks learned that I was a Kazakh, they said, "We share the same blood with you." Many Turks still call Kazakhstan "Zher Ana"—Motherland, the country of their ancestors. Will Turkic missionaries, former Muslims, be successful in Turkey?

When you return home, you will have a reason to rejoice, just as John the Baptist did. "The bride belongs to the bridegroom. The friend who attends the bridegroom waits and listens for him, and is full of joy when he hears the bridegroom's voice. That joy is mine, and it is now complete."[121]

In his commentary on the third chapter of the Gospel of John, William Barclay, wrote:

> The friend of the bridegroom, the shoshben, had a unique place at a Jewish wedding. He acted as the liaison between the bride and the bridegroom; he arranged the wedding; he took out the invitations; he presided at the wedding feast. He brought the bride and the bridegroom together. And he had one special duty. It was his duty to guard the bridal chamber and to let no false lover in. He would open the door only when in the dark he heard the bridegroom's voice and recognized it. When he heard the bridegroom's voice he let him in and went away rejoicing, for his task was completed and the lovers were together. He did not grudge the bridegroom the bride. He knew that his only task had been to bring bride and bridegroom together. And when that task was done, he willingly and gladly faded out of the centre of the picture.[122]

---

121   John 3:29
122   William Barclay, "Commentary on John 3," *William Barclay's Daily Study Bible*, https://www.studylight.org/commentaries/dsb/john-3.html, 1956-1959.

# CHAPTER 11

# ANOTHER PERSPECTIVE

IN THE SOVIET FILM BY Stanislav Govorukhin, *The Meeting Place Cannot be Changed* (a film about the struggle of police officers against the criminal gangs that emerged after World War II), there is a scene when the young investigator Sharapov talks about his military experience:

> When I commanded a reconnaissance unit at the front, I would often send a fresh person to be a lookout. One who had been on guard for a while would report whatever he saw, but the new one would look at things with a fresh eye. And you know what? Sometimes it was very good. After many hours, an observer's eyes could become "clouded" because of the stress of an entire day on watch. He saw things that weren't there but didn't see things that might appear unexpectedly.[123]

Remember the ancient Indian parable "The Elephant and the Blind Men"? One blind man touched the side of an elephant and said, "The elephant is a big wall." Another grabbed his trunk. "No. He looks like a snake." The third touched a leg and said, "This is a tree."

If I was Ryan from Iowa and came to Kazakhstan as a missionary, how would I advise myself? Let me tell you my truth about the "elephant."

## TOURISTS IN THE FIELD OF GOD

Let's start with "The Calling." Has God called you to be a messenger? There are many other reasons to become a missionary:

---

123   *Meeting Place Cannot Be Changed*, Directed by Stanislaw Govorukhin, the U.S.S.R., 1979.

- A Desire to See the World

In a documentary I watched, a soldier was asked, "Why did you join the army?" He replied, "I went to serve because I want to study the world and travel. I have visited Germany, Panama, North Carolina, and Afghanistan."[124] Not the best reason to become a soldier.

- Guilt Avoidance

I once asked a missionary, "Why did you become a missionary?" He replied that he lived in a big house on the ocean, worked for a large company, had a big salary, had a beautiful car . . . I listened to him for a long time, paying close attention; he didn't speak about his calling; it was all about his guilt.

- Emotions-driven

The science of emotional intelligence says that people manage organizations, companies, and states; but emotions drive people. Early books on trade taught that purchases are the result of calculation and logic. Recent research on sales psychology suggests otherwise. People may make a purchase based on irrational motives; maybe they liked the seller, were attracted to the story, or were just in a good mood. In the morning, women return clothes to malls because the music of George Michael and Stevie Wonder was not playing at home.

You can hear an inspiring sermon or read a stirring book and be motivated to become a missionary. There is nothing wrong with that, but that is not a calling. I have already mentioned the story of the possessed man and the pigs in the Gospel of Mark. The narrative ends with the man who formerly lived in graves asking to follow Jesus. He is amazed; his heart is full of feelings; he feels good with this Man.

---

124  Realization of Truth, "Strange – Goodbye America – Myths of Power," YouTube video, 48:26, August 7, 2012, https://www.youtube.com/watch?v=1JspN7k7UBM.

But "Jesus did not let him."[125] God can use emotions on the way to your calling, but emotions themselves are not a calling. Emotions will pass, but the armed streets of Kabul will remain.

- To Find Meaning in Life

Everyone who is following Christ wants to live for something more and find their own meaning in life. It is right. But don't confuse "calling" and "meaning in life." They are two separate concepts. And meaning can be found in your hometown—not just in a foreign country.

## CALLED TO THE FIELD OF GOD

The word *missionary* is the equivalent of the word *apostle* in the New Testament. What does it mean? Simply, a messenger. Let's look at the most famous messenger of the New Testament, the apostle Paul. How did he view missionary work?

- "Paul, a servant of Christ Jesus, called to be an apostle and set apart for the gospel of God" (Rom. 1:1)
- "Paul, called to be an apostle of Christ Jesus by the will of God" (1 Cor. 1:1)
- "Paul, an apostle of Christ Jesus by the will of God" (2 Cor. 1:1)
- "Paul, an apostle—sent not from men nor by man, but by Jesus Christ and God the Father, who raised him from the dead" (Gal. 1:1)
- "Paul, an apostle of Christ Jesus by the will of God, To God's holy people in Ephesus, the faithful in Christ Jesus" (Eph. 1:1)
- "Paul, an apostle of Christ Jesus by the will of God, and Timothy our brother" (Col. 1:1)
- "Paul, an apostle of Christ Jesus by the command of God our Savior and of Christ Jesus our hope" (1 Tim. 1:1)

- "Paul, an apostle of Christ Jesus by the will of God, in keeping with the promise of life that is in Christ Jesus" (2 Tim. 1:1)
- "Paul, a servant of God and an apostle of Jesus Christ" (Titus 1:1)

Paul hammers this idea into us. At the beginning of these letters, every time Paul uses the word "apostle," he adds "called" or "by the will of God." As a river cannot exist without banks, Paul cannot use the word apostle without adding "by the will of God." Even in Titus, he adds "the apostle of Jesus Christ."

He practically cries out, "I am not a tourist; I am here with a purpose. I did not attain this position by myself, or deserve it, or appoint myself; no, I was sent by God." People do not become missionaries because they were sent by Navigators or graduated from the Moody Bible Institute. You can have ten diplomas with the title "missionary," and this will not help you. For all the wonderful efforts of missionary schools, the teachings of famous professors, and millions in donations, the last word remains with God—"not from men nor by a man."[126]

Not everyone will be like Matthew, who actually saw Him say "follow Me" and then left his tax collector's table. Not everyone will physically hear a Voice from Heaven like Paul, but everyone should still be listening for the Voice.

## HOW TO HEAR THE VOICE OF GOD

I am not an expert in this topic; I am just a beginner. There are recognized experts who can say more: Charles Stanley, Jack Deere, John Wimber. That said, I want to share some points that help me in this matter. The most interesting passage in Scripture on the topic is found in 1 Samuel 3:1-9:

> The boy Samuel ministered before the LORD under Eli. In those days the word of the LORD was rare; there were not many visions. One night Eli, whose eyes were becoming so weak that he could barely see, was lying down in his usual place. The lamp of God

had not yet gone out, and Samuel was lying down in the house of the LORD, where the ark of God was. Then the LORD called Samuel. Samuel answered, "Here I am." And he ran to Eli and said, "Here I am; you called me."

But Eli said, "I did not call; go back and lie down." So he went and lay down.

Again, the LORD called, "Samuel!" And Samuel got up and went to Eli and said, "Here I am; you called me."

"My son," Eli said, "I did not call; go back and lie down."

Now Samuel did not yet know the LORD: The word of the LORD had not yet been revealed to him.

A third time the LORD called, "Samuel!" And Samuel got up and went to Eli and said, "Here I am; you called me."

Then Eli realized that the LORD was calling the boy. So Eli told Samuel, "Go and lie down, and if he calls you, say, 'Speak, LORD, for your servant is listening.'" So Samuel went and lay down in his place.

I like this passage, since Samuel had then the same problem as we do today:

## HOW TO DISTINGUISH GOD'S VOICE FROM A HUMAN VOICE

Imagine your colleague brings you a backpack and says, "When we celebrated the anniversary of our company, one of us forgot their backpack at the restaurant. Do you know whose backpack this is? Maybe it's yours?"

Looking at the backpack, you can't exactly determine whose backpack it is; maybe it belongs to Matt, Joshua, or Cindy, but you can definitely say whether or not it's your backpack. So it is in hearing the voice of God. You need to know what your "backpack" looks like; you need to understand the nature of your own voice.

By the way, when I say God's voice, I do not mean an audible voice that we hear with our ears, but rather what we hear on the inside. Samuel heard God—outside of himself, with his ears. In those days, the Lord dwelt in the temple of God. Now, we are the temple of God, and God dwells in us. Therefore, this Voice lives within us. This we hear not with the ear but with the heart.

In time, I began to understand the nature of my voice, my thoughts. I know that I think slowly, so I hate tests and interviews with questions that need to be answered right away. Sometimes, when I'm not even praying, a question appears in my spirit, and the answer appears instantly. I know that this is not me.

I once read Jack Deere's book *Surprised by the Voice of God*. After reading the chapter in which he talks about the gift of prophecy, I stood in front of the wall and prayed, "God, give me the gift of prophecy." I did not even have time to utter the word "prophecy" when the question came: "Why?" Inside, everything went cold. First of all, I knew for sure that it was not me. I can't think that fast. Second, the question really hit me. I thought, *What is my true motive? Why do I need the gift of prophecy? To be cool? To entertain others? To have something others don't have?* By constant practice, a person begins to understand which voice is theirs and which is not.

I have two sons. The oldest is eight years old; the youngest is five. When they shout from the second floor, I distinguish their voices. My eldest son says little; but when he speaks, he speaks deliberately, often asking interesting questions: "Why do we believe in one God and our neighbors in another?" "Do black holes exist in outer space?" Once we flew on a plane, and each of us was given a lunch. He asked, "Why did everyone get a packet of sugar, even though not everyone eats sugar?" "Dad, how many planes does this airline have?"

My youngest son rarely asks questions, though he talks a lot. Most often, he complains or makes excuses why it's not his fault that something has been broken. I can distinguish them by the timbre and rhythm of their voices. The older speaks softly, slowly, and quietly; the younger speaks forcefully, loudly, and quickly.

In years past, computers could not play two media files at the same time. Nowadays, I sometimes forget to turn off "Happy" by Pharrell Williams and also hear Thanos fighting Iron Man. Once I was thinking of an idea and then heard a parallel audio track in my head that seemed to be on top of my own thoughts. I know that I am an old PC, unable to play two tracks. The most interesting thing is that this second track was on a different topic. I understood that this other track was not me because it is difficult for me to focus even on one thought.

Continuing the conversation about the nature of the Voice, we return to 1 Kings 19:12b: "after the fire came a gentle whisper." There is no better comparison, symbol, or metaphor for the voice of the Holy Spirit. He really is like a quiet wind. Of all the voices heard inside you, this is the most calm and quiet. This Voice is not in a hurry because He is always on time. Therefore, it is important to develop a spiritual sensitivity to this Voice.

This year, we enrolled our daughter in a music school where she studies various disciplines. One of them is solfeggio, an academic discipline for the development of musical hearing and memory. This helps young musicians distinguish and analyze different tonalities, rhythms, intervals, and chords. In the same way, we need to have our solfeggio of the Holy Spirit which will help us to distinguish the whispering wind from other winds. I would like this Voice to be louder and more forceful, but He is what He is. I cannot control Him.

And this brings us to another topic.

## WE CANNOT CONTROL THE WHISPERING WIND

Have you ever thought that for many people, Marvel's superheroes are preferable to biblical heroes? There may be many reasons for this, but I want to draw attention to one advantage. Each of these superheroes controls their gift at will. Some examples: Wolverine has the ability to regenerate and has six blades in his hands; Mystic has the gift of reincarnation; Magneto controls magnetic fields; Storm has power over the weather. They had to learn how to control their own power, which Professor Charles Xavier helped them to do. Once they learned, they could manage their gift at any time, at will.

In the Bible, the apostle Paul could resurrect a man but could not heal himself of a disease (the "thorn in [his] flesh"[127]). King David killed Goliath with a stone, yet another time, he fled from Saul and pretended to be insane. Samson killed one thousand Philistines with a donkey's jawbone; but when they cut his hair and the Lord left him, they put out his eyes and chained him up.

Before Elijah was to be taken to Heaven, he asked Elisha, "'Tell me, what can I do for you before I am taken from you?' 'Let me inherit a double portion of your spirit,' Elisha replied. 'You have asked a difficult thing,' Elijah said, 'yet if you see me when I am taken from you, it will be yours—otherwise, it will not.'"[128] Before leaving his beloved student, Elijah wanted to do something good for him. He wanted to bless and, as a father, leave an inheritance to his son. In other words, he says, "Ask whatever you want." But when Elisha asked, Elijah understood that this request was beyond his power.

Unlike superheroes who control their power, biblical heroes cannot rule God. God rules them. It is the same for us. We cannot command God and cannot make Him speak. We can only ask, and as Jesus said, "It will be given to you."[129] We can only wait, like David: "In the morning, LORD, you hear my voice; in the morning I lay my requests before you and wait expectantly."[130] We can learn to listen like Samuel did when he was just a boy.

*"The wind blows wherever it pleases. You hear its sound, but you cannot tell where it comes from or where it is going. So it is with everyone born of the Spirit."*[131]

You cannot control His voice; you can only hear Him when He wants to be heard. There are days when I can hear Him several times throughout the day. Sometimes, there is some kind of amazing communication between

---

127   2 Corinthians 12:7
128   2 Kings 2:9-10
129   Matthew 7:7
130   Psalm 5:3
131   John 3:8

my spirit and God's Spirit, which is difficult to describe. It's not a prayer or a petition, but a thought arises in my spirit and then another thought. These thoughts fit together like pieces of a puzzle. This is very similar to what the psalmist described: "Deep calls to deep in the roar of your waterfalls."[132] I do not participate; I stand on the bank and watch the water fall into the river.

Sometimes for weeks, I may hear nothing. It doesn't at all mean that God has stopped speaking. God continues to speak on various subjects, but God is not answering my most pressing questions or life concerns. Even in this situation, His silence can be very loud. Then I understand the lines, "My God, my God, why have you forsaken me? Why are you so far from saving me, so far from my cries of anguish? My God, I cry out by day, but you do not answer, by night, but I find no rest."[133] He will choose the time and method of His answering.

He can also answer before you ask. Or He can answer two weeks later, right in the middle of a meeting where the head of the company is giving a report on quarterly sales of pharmaceutical products.

It will not always be an internal voice. God can answer through your brother, through an advertisement on a passing bus, in a dream or vision, through CNN news, or through Scripture. Ultimately, the Old and New Testament are the main source of God's voice. I like what Priscilla Shirer said in a TV interview: "We have discounted the power of Scripture, because if we say that we want to hear from God and we never read the love letter that He wrote for us, we don't want to really hear from God."[134] At that moment, the Holy Spirit will prompt, "This is it."

I wrote earlier about the difficult period of my life after I left the mission. Nobody needed my previous experience; I failed at everything. Then my friend Ruslan suggested contacting a member of his church, a Singaporean who taught personal growth. When I met with him, he told me that he did

---

132  Psalm 42:7
133  Psalm 22:1-2
134  Priscilla Shirer, "Priscilla Shirer: Discerning the Voice of God | Praise on TBN," 4:28, Praise on TBN, October 22, 2020, https://www.youtube.com/watch?v=FaZ8SlAcCVk.

not need a trainer but was looking for a translator. I came home and told my wife, "Despite our financial difficulties, this job is not for me. I'm not a translator. The salary he offered will cover only half of our expenses. And if I work with him, I work *only* for him; I won't be able to work two jobs."

God blessed me with a wife who agrees with me in everything. But inside I heard, "Now that you have asked your wife for her opinion about this job, do you want to hear Mine?"

After dinner, I went to be alone and asked God, "Is it Your will that I start working with this person?" I waited for a long time but heard nothing. I tried to hear with my heart and not with my mind, just as I was taught in books on hearing God's voice. I tried to calm my mind. I tried to just wait. I was running around the house; I prayed standing up; I prayed on my knees with my eyes open and with my eyes closed, but nothing happened.

At the end of the prayer, I was kneeling in the living room with my eyes closed and said, "I did everything I could. I heard nothing. The end." I opened my eyes and saw before me a toybox with a children's backpack sticking out of the top, on which, in huge block letters, I saw the name of the person who had offered me the job. A cold chill ran through me when I saw this, as if an angel were in front of me with wings filling the entire room. I took it for an answer.

After many years of thinking about this experience, I am even more convinced this was His voice. That year was one of the most difficult in my life but also one of the most fruitful. Up until that year, I was like a runner from James Dashner's *Maze Runner*. I did not remember how I got there and did not know how to get out. At the beginning of the year, I set exactly the same goals that I had set the year before. I once had a dream that accurately described my life: I was in a small room which had no windows or doors, only walls. When I looked up, I saw the sky; there was no roof. There, high up above, I saw a man reach out his hand to me, but the distance was too great. Finally, that year, I received a map to my maze.

A few months prior, my eldest son was diagnosed with a serious heart condition. I did not ask God why this happened. Inside, there was a simple understanding that this was not an accident. It was a part of His will. God has a plan, but it was hard on my heart. My wife was crying.

Two days after getting this news, my family and I went to see the animated movie *Ralph Breaks the Internet*. When Ralph and Vanellope have a falling out, Shank comforts Vanellope, saying, "At some point, all friendships are tested."[135] All the audience in the theater heard those words, but I heard, "Kanat, our friendship is being tested." And even more: "Now you have touched a little bit on what I went through with respect to My Son."

God can speak in varied and unexpected ways. In my relationship with God, I realize that He is a very creative Person. He does not use templates and ready-made schemes. Sometimes, though, we do not accept such a voice.

Can God speak through a Disney cartoon, a book by Charles Dickens, a neighbor, or a TV advertisement?

We think that if something comes from God, it should at least resemble thunder from Heaven (well, it may also come through a pastor or the Bible), but the Holy Spirit uses simple things that surround us. Does this remind you of anyone? Jesus did the same. The Savior always taught the disciples using common things or what they saw along their way. He saw birds and said: "Look at the birds of the air; they do not sow or reap or store away in barns, and yet your heavenly Father feeds them. Are you not much more valuable than they?"[136] He would pass a mountain and say, "If anyone says to this mountain, 'Go, throw yourself into the sea,' and does not doubt in their heart but believes that what they say will happen, it will be done for him."[137]

Sometimes, you don't need a voice. God may provide a certain wisdom regarding how to act in a given situation. And by the way, don't go to the

135  "Ralph Breaks the Internet," directed by Rich Moore and Phil Johnston, Burbank, CA: Walt Disney Feature Animation, 2018.
136  Matthew 6:26
137  Mark 11:23

other extreme: Some who previously had not listened to God are now trying to hear Him in every little thing. Say you are going on a missionary trip to Russia; you don't need to ask God whether to take a jacket. For this, you have a weather forecast.

We have two kinds of choices to make: one is moral, and the other is practical. For moral choices, we need not ask God, for He has given us Scripture for this. You do not need to ask God, "Can I watch erotic films, or should I spend more time with my children, or did You call me to serve?" The answers are obvious. The better you know the Scripture, the easier it is to answer this type of question. But there are questions related to the course of our lives for which Scripture does not give an answer. The Holy Spirit is within us for these kinds of questions: Is Robert the husband God has prepared for me? Does God call me to quit my job as a programmer and become a missionary? Which seminary would be the best choice for me, Gordon Conwell or Fuller?

Also, often we will not need to ask God because wisdom grows within us as we consistently meditate on Scripture, learn to hear and obey Him, make mistakes, and live life with Him.

I like the French film *The Chef,* starring Jean Reno and Michaël Youn. A young chef, Jacky Bonnot, can't keep a job because he wants to develop a taste for fine dining among the patrons of cheap cafés. He wants to cook "pumpkin mousse paternat with chestnut jelly and ravioli with tomato on oak leaves" instead of "chops and fries." For the sake of his pregnant wife, Jacky finds a job as house painter in a nursing home, where he also helps in the kitchen. Alexandre Lagarde, a famous chef, holder of Michelin stars, offers him a job as an assistant. After hesitating, Jacky accepts the invitation. Since childhood, Jacky admired the work of Alexandre; he compares his recipes with the works of Michelangelo. Once, in the nursing home, he and the other cooks watched a cooking show where Lagarde shared the secret of making puree soup with leeks. Jacky noticed something strange: "He didn't use onion in the recipe, and that means he has a problem—at work or with a woman."

One of the cooks asked, "Do you know him?" "By heart. When things were hard for me, I used to give myself his books."

When they began working together, Jacky, during the absence of Alexandre, changed one of the recipes; he added cinnamon to the lamb sauce.

During a quarrel, Jacky shouted at Alexandre, "I know how Alexandre worked."

"But I am Alexandre."

"I was Alexandre from the very beginning."[138]

Like Jacky, who became like Alexandre, we become more like our God. "And we all, who with unveiled faces contemplate the Lord's glory, are being transformed into his image with ever-increasing glory, which comes from the Lord, who is the Spirit."[139]

## WHEN GOD SPEAKS, HE EXPECTS HIS WORDS TO BE APPLIED

At the end of the eighteenth century in London, a commoner, fascinated by mathematics but not having the opportunity to study at Oxford, was determined to access books. The poor, unhappy man was not permitted to enter the library, but by chance, he learned of a professor, a good-hearted man, who had his own private library containing books by Descartes, Newton, and Euler. In shabby clothes and with cap in hand, he nervously knocked on the door of the mansion and explained to the owner the purpose of his visit. The professor was indignant, offended—what an idea! These books were more precious than gold; this was his life's collection, where he invested most of his university salary; these books were his true wealth. Just to wipe dust from them brought incomparable pleasure, not to mention owning them. However, the poor man continued to make his requests, and the professor decided to loan one book: *New Method for Maximums and Minimums* by Leibniz. The commoner left very satisfied. A month later, he returned.

---

138 "Comme un chef," directed by Daniel Kohen, Neuilly-sur-Seine, France: Gaumont, 2012.
139 2 Corinthians 3:18

"Ah, you have already mastered Leibniz," said the professor.

"No," the poor man scratched his head. "I have not started reading it yet, but I thought . . . could you give me something by Euler?"

Isn't this like us? We have been asking God for a long time to speak to us, and when He speaks, we say, "Ah, I see. Maybe you could say something else?" God does not speak for the sake of entertainment. When He speaks, His words have meaning; they are His will for our life. The Professor is unlikely to give the commoner another book.

The eminent theologian Karl Barth, of whom even Russian Orthodox theologians speak as a last Father of the Church—the likes of whom will never be seen again, wrote thirteen volumes on church dogmatics. In an interview with a German television channel, Barth said, "He is not a dead God, as some fools say today. He is the living God who continues to speak. If we have ears to hear, we can hear Him constantly."[140]

Why did Eli realize only the third time that it was God? Because he had long forgotten what the voice of God sounded like. Eli was the symbol of a generation that had forgotten the voice of God. Samuel represented a new generation, one that learned to hear Him. To which generation do we belong?

The ability to hear God is not only needed to find a calling. For me, this is the most important skill of a minister. In his book *Experiencing God: Knowing and Doing the Will of God*, Henry Blackaby presents a fundamental principle: Watch to see where God is working and join Him.[141] "The Son can do nothing by himself; he can do nothing by himself; he can do only what he sees his Father doing, because whatever the Father does the Son also does."[142] The idea itself is simple, but it's not so easy to see where God is and what He is doing. Here, the skill of hearing God's voice is invaluable.

---

140  "JA und NEIN, Karl Barth zum Gedaechtnis," directed by Heinz Knorr Stuttgart, Baden-Württemberg, Germany: Calwer Verlag, 1967.

141  Henry Blackaby, *Experiencing God: Knowing and Doing the Will of God* (Nashville: B&H Books, Revised Edition, 2008).

142  John 5:19

## TRYING IS NOT TORTURE

There is a tool that will help establish us in our vocation. This tool is called Try.

When I was in school, I read a biography of Mike Tyson and desired to become a boxer. I dreamed about it for many months and thought how cool it would be to become an Olympic champion. I must say that Kazakhstan has a very strong boxing tradition. Over the past twenty years, Kazakhstan has produced seven Olympic champions.[143] In 2018, Gennady Golovkin (GGG) was rated as the best professional boxer regardless of weight category by the magazine *The Ring*; Wladimir Klitschko (Dr. Steelhammer) held the world heavyweight title for twelve years, longer than any other in the history of the heavyweight division, and was born in Kazakhstan.

When I came to the boxing gym at the age of fourteen, they explained that I had come too late. I should have started boxing at seven or eight years of age. But since I insisted, they took me. After three months of training, I realized that I didn't want to be a boxer. I don't like to run kilometers in the morning. I don't want to beat the speed bag for hours while learning proper breathing; I don't have a fighting spirit. I didn't look like the boys who "lived" there. When I arrived, they were there; when I left, they were there. They were not interested in computer games, TV, or girls. The coach made them each bring a report card from school and show their grades because some did not want to go to school. For them, school was just time they were not in the ring.

Now, when I lead the department of training and personal development in a large company, young people are interested in things like, "How to Become Successful" and "How to Start a Business." Many of them think that the most important things when creating a business are either start-up capital or an idea or finding an investor. To which I say, those things are way down the list. I continue, "If you want to open a restaurant, don't lose ten years searching for start-up capital; rent a hole in the wall and sell shawarma."

---

143  Seven gold medalists; counting silver and bronze, the number is more than twenty.

When you open your first business, your main task is not to earn money but rather to understand whether or not you are a businessman. This is the million-dollar question. The tragedy of entrepreneurs is that they may spend many years searching for start-up capital, finding a brilliant idea, or getting an education. Some people think that to become an entrepreneur, you need to get an MBA, then a DBA, and then an MBA at Stanford. Yet when they finally start their own business, after the first year, they understand that they don't like being an entrepreneur. They don't like creating a budget; they don't like selling; they don't like starting from scratch; they don't like building a team; they don't like to take risks. All this can be learned without getting an MBA at Stanford.

You may feel that God called you to become a missionary but have your doubts. You have two options: either dream for a lifetime or become a missionary for a year. In one year, you will learn more than the greatest mission school can teach you in ten years.

A strong sense of calling will definitely help when you leave the USA (or any other first-world country). When Americans ask me what I think about the USA, I say, "Heaven on earth." The police do not stop you and extort money; you can buy Levi's jeans for twenty dollars; you can swim at a beach, and no one will tell you that it's their beach. Some Americans think they have bad roads. I tell them, "You have never seen bad roads." When you arrive in a country where there is no water in the faucet, where people are more afraid of the police than of thugs, where a landlord can receive the first month's rent and evict you the next day (you can certainly go to court, but it may turn out that the judge is the landlord who evicted you), then you understand that you are in a completely different galaxy with its own set of laws. This is when your sense of calling gives strength.

The author of *The Song of Ice and Fire*, George Martin, give this advice to novice writers: "Ask yourself, if no one ever bought any of my work? What if I'm never going to sell a book or publish a book or a short story? Are you going continue to write? If the answer's yes, because I have to, then you are a writer."[144] The Moravian Brethren, when commissioning missionaries, asked this: Are you willing to go, die, and be forgotten?[145] If the answer is yes, then you are a missionary. Despite a real danger to your life or lack of money, you would never trade your calling for anything in the world.

## DON'T GREET ANYONE ON THE WAY

In chapter ten of the Gospel of Luke, Jesus gives instruction to the seventy-two. One of the directions seems strange: "Do not greet anyone on the way."[146] Shouldn't we be friendly and good to people? Didn't Jesus say, "Love your neighbor as yourself?"[147]

To understand this instruction, we need to understand the culture of relationships in Israel at that time. When travelers were on the road, they passed villages, cities, and dwellings. In front of the dwellings and at the gates of cities were men talking or resting from work. If a traveler was in a hurry, then he paid no attention to anything except the dust under his feet. Seeing he was in a hurry, no one would talk to him—perhaps he was going to the temple, maybe to pray, maybe going home to his wife and children. But if the traveler greeted someone with "Sholem Aleichem" (peace to this house), then he showed that he was ready for fellowship and was not in a hurry.

Hospitality is an important commandment in Judaism. The rabbis said, "The merit of one who receives guests is similar to the merit of one who in the morning hurries to the house of learning."[148] Therefore, an orthodox Jew was obligated to invite the traveler into his house, give him a chance to rest, feed him, offer wine, even bathe him and welcome him to spend the night. This

144 Evan Carmichael, "George R. R. Martin's Top 10 Rules For Success (@GRRM-speaking)," December 21, 2016, YouTube video, 24:05, https://www.youtube.com/watch?v=gSZkktU7ylA.

145 Janet and Geoff Benge, *Count Zinzendorf: Firstfruit* (Christian Heroes: Then & Now) (Edmonds: YWAM Publishing, 2006).

146 Luke 10:4b

147 Mark 12:31

148 Yitzchak Silver,*Paths of Peace and Goodness*, eds. Zvi Wasserman and Leia Shukhman (Russia, 2012).

would distract the disciples from their mission. They would receive all of this, but only upon reaching their destination.

This admonition of Christ is more relevant to our time than ever. Many things in the modern world fight for our attention. These distractions turn us from the most important thing in life, the mission God has given us.

### FUN MINISTRY

While working on his novel *Madame Bovary*, Gustave Flaubert, one of the greatest European writers of the nineteenth century, wrote:

> My head is spinning from anguish, discontentment and fatigue. I sat over the manuscript for the whole four hours and could not compose a single phrase. Today I haven't written a single decent line, but I have scribbled a hundred shoddy ones. What awful labor! What a pain! Oh art, my art! What is this monstrous chimera that eats away at our hearts, and what for? It is pure madness to doom yourself to such suffering.[149] [150]

To drown out the pain, some writers create various distractions—they meet with readers, appear on television programs, teach writing skills. They do anything to avoid actually writing. This can also happen with a missionary. You invite people to your home, but they don't come; you preach the Gospel, but people don't repent; you've spent four years in the country, and there are three people in your church, not counting you, your wife, and children. Then you are tempted to "not write" and to replace it with something similar.

For example, say your friend with whom you studied at seminary, now pastor of a church in Louisville, Kentucky, invites you to teach a course on missions at his church. You gladly accept the invitation. Then you hear that in two months, there will be a great conference in Vietnam dedicated to evangelizing Muslims. You start packing your bags. Then you have a grand

---

149   Jan Parandowski, *Alchemy of the Word* (Moscow: Progress Publishing, 1972).
150   Translated from Russian.

idea: to continue your theological education in Nevada (after all, you can't have too much knowledge!), and it won't take too much time; you have to be there just twice a year. In the fall, the Central Asian Partnership meets in Turkey. And so on . . .

Soon, you have from eight to ten trips a year, yet you are still the pastor of a church in Dushanbe, Tajikistan. At every conference, seminar, or Bible school, you passionately share how you reach people for Christ in Tajikistan. I have a question: where do you reach them? In the fuselage? On board, between New York and Amsterdam? I've attended conferences where some ministers boasted that after this conference, they would fly directly to another conference.

This disease also affects local leaders, who can more often be seen at an international seminar than in their own church. I am sure that if you invite local pastors to a Christian conference in Denver, Colorado, or Paris, France, with all expenses paid, eighty percent will agree without even knowing the topic. Though their church is in a Muslim environment, they will explain to their members the importance of the topic "10 Principles of Evangelizing Buddhists." Furthermore, after six months, they will describe the Triumphal Arch in full detail but are unlikely to remember the principles.

I'm not saying that attending conferences or seminars is bad. They are necessary for a missionary or a minister. When I served in the mission, I thought we had too many conferences. Now, after six years of being an "independent" minister (independent in the sense that not much depends on me) and not attending a single conference or seminar in all that time, I have begun to understand their meaning and purpose. A conference is a place where you do not teach but are taught, where you do not encourage but are encouraged, where you can just take a break from the pressures of ministry, pray with the brothers and drink tea (perhaps, in your case, coffee) maybe one or two times a year. But when you go somewhere, always ask yourself this question: Does this conference help me in Tajikistan (Lithuania, Bangladesh, Thailand,

Argentina, etc.), or is it just fun—it's a lot of fun to visit different countries and post pictures on Facebook—or is it merely an imitation of hectic activity?

## ISOLATION IN YOUR COMMUNITY

Don't create a "Little America" within Kazakhstan: your children go to an American school; on Sundays, you attend an American church; you have a missionary home group meeting on Wednesday nights. To complete your happiness, Papa Johns and Starbucks materialized in Kazakhstan. But ask this question, "Have you forgotten what you came for?"

I have already mentioned my missionary friend, Charles. Well, he is not a typical missionary. He has lived in Kazakhstan for more than twenty years and doesn't have his own house; he rents an apartment. He has a wife and three children and has never owned a car. He is an example among Kazakhs of what it to be very hospitable. He also has a rule: he and his family try not to communicate with foreigners, believers or non-believers; they don't visit them, don't spend time with them, don't participate in their communities. For twenty years, they have not forgotten why they are here.

## LACK OF ACTION

The concept "We are not responsible for results; only God is responsible for results" is widely held in missionary circles. It seems to me that a misunderstanding of this idea leads ministers to a lack of action. Yes, you cannot guarantee that ten people will come to Christ this month, but you can say that you will share the Gospel with ten people. You cannot guarantee that God will answer your prayer, but you can be diligent in prayer and seek the face of the Lord.

I once cried out to God and complained that no one came to Him, that nobody needs Jesus in Kazakhstan, that people are blind and do not see His love and grace, that they do not want to be saved. Then I heard the still voice of the Holy Spirit say, "How many people have you shared the Gospel with this month?"

You may hear someone say, "At least, I was not deported." Do you think the local KGB[151] doesn't know about your existence? Maybe your "wise" ministry does not bother them at all. It is so "wise" that your mission leadership, after listening to a two-hour presentation, cannot understand what you are doing in the country where you were sent. I am not saying that you should arrive in country and the next day preach a sermon at the central mosque. But you need to honestly admit what is caution and what is fear, what is patience and what is laziness, and where stupidity is shielded by the word "prudence."

Psalm 90:12 says, "Teach us to number our days, that we may gain a heart of wisdom." Wisdom is being honest with yourself. If you have a wife and four children, you don't count ten individual years that have passed but sixty years of your entire family's life combined. To explain it in corporate terms, if a company sent ten sales managers for a one-day conference, each manager accounts for eight hours, but the company invested eighty hours total. How do you want to spend this time? Perhaps as the "wise minnow," from a fairy tale by Mikhail Saltykov-Shchedrin, who did not want to lose his life and so constantly sat in a burrow and lived to be one hundred years old. At the end of his life, he thought, "Should a minnow's life have been like this?"[152] Is "saving a visa" an end in itself?

Is it easier to work for yourself or for someone else? It's much easier to work for someone else. When I work for a corporation, I have a timecard that records when I arrive and when I leave. If I miss a couple of hours, a manager will always ask where I've been. Ultimately, they can fire me. When I was self-employed, I could spend the whole day watching *Friends* on TV and then mark it on the calendar as "Learning English." Similarly, a missionary can have fun all day long with his local friends and then call it "evangelism."

Some of my friends, Cru missionaries in the city, have their own team and meet periodically to ask each other difficult questions. A local leader may ask

---

151   Like the FBI in America; the national security organization
152   Michail Saltykov–Shchedrin, "Wise minnow," *Fairy Tales\\ Collected Works in Twenty Volumes,* Vol. 16 (Moscow, 1974).

the missionaries questions or vice versa. They are free to say anything they think. Of course, they have to be very accurate, not blame one another, be honest, and not make personal attacks. They may ask, "Would you be able to share the Gospel this month?," "Do your activities advance your objectives?," or "How is your personal relationship with Christ?" After these meetings, sometimes people may have conflict or even be offended. But it's a good time because people receive honest feedback.

What about when you don't have such a team, when are you alone in the city? Nobody knows when you get up, what you do, or who you meet. I think those of us who work for a corporation should work as if serving in a mission, and those who serve in the ministry should work as if working for a corporation.

Without hard work, it's impossible to achieve anything of significance. I have studied the issue of success for more than fifteen years within the context of church history as well as other areas of human activity. I studied the life stories of the apostle Paul, Francis Xavier, Saint Augustine, C. S. Lewis, Leonardo da Vinci, Michelangelo, Leo Tolstoy, Vincent Van Gogh, Mohamed Ali, Sam Walton, and Ray Kroc. There are many myths about successful people. These days, we see a lot of articles with names like *7 Habits of Successful People* or *Morning Rituals of Big Businessmen*. If you carefully study the biographies of famous people, it's clear that many articles are far from the truth. For example, it has been said that "all successful people get up early and sleep little." Gustav Flaubert woke up at ten a.m; after serving in the army, F. Scott Fitzgerald got up at eleven o'clock and went to bed late; Albert Einstein and Arthur Schopenhauer slept for ten hours a day.

What about, "Successful people play sports and lead a healthy lifestyle?" Jean-Paul Sartre worked hard, slept little, drank a lot, smoked, and later took methamphetamine. British Prime Minister Winston Churchill was overweight, loved Armenian cognac and Scotch whiskey, and smoked Cuban cigars. I don't want to say that you should lead an unhealthy life. I'm just showing the fact that someone could be a great politician and at the same time not lead a very healthy life.

"Successful people are financially independent." The painting *Irises* by Vincent Van Gogh sold for 101.2 million dollars at Sotheby's auction. However, Van Gogh sold only one painting during his lifetime and would trade a painting for a kilo of potatoes; his brother supported him all his life. When the writer Vladimir Nabokov arrived in Berlin, he gave boxing lessons to make ends meet.

However, I can agree with this: all successful people, regardless of culture, epoch, or field of activity, have worked hard. Here is an excerpt from Mason Currey's book *Daily Rituals: How Artists Work* in which he writes of Voltaire:

> A visitor recorded Voltaire's routine in 1774: He spent the morning in bed, reading and dictating new work to one of his secretaries. At noon he rose and got dressed. Then he would receive visitors or, if there were none, continue to work, taking coffee and chocolate for sustenance. (He did not eat lunch.) Between 2:00 and 4:00, Voltaire and his principal secretary, Jean-Louis Wagnière, went out in a carriage to survey the estate. Then he worked again until 8:00, when he would join his widowed niece Madame Denis and others for supper. But his working day did not end there. Voltaire often continued to give dictation after supper, continuing deep into the night. Wagnière estimated that, all told, they worked eighteen to twenty hours a day.[153]

Everyone has heard the saying of Thomas Edison, "Genius is one percent inspiration, ninety-nine percent perspiration." But there is another quote: "I never did a day's work in my life; it was all fun." No one doubts that Edison worked hard. Virtuoso pianist Denis Matsuev played 264 concerts in 2016. Describing his busy schedule, he says, "I already know what will happen in 2022." Basketball star Kobe Bryant conducts three workouts a day. The owner of the largest grocery store chain in Manhattan, John Catsimatidis, was asked,

---

153  Currey, ibid.

"What's the one thing every first-time entrepreneur should know?" He replied, "Be prepared for personal sacrifice. Be prepared to work 24/7 to win. If you are not willing to do this . . . keep your day job."[154]

Just as one cannot become a successful businessman, composer, or sportsman without hard work, one cannot become a "successful" missionary, evangelist, or pastor without working hard.

Charles Spurgeon, in his book *Lectures to My Students*, writes, "We are few, and we have a desperate fight before us, therefore it is needful that every man should be made the most of, and nerved to his highest point of strength."[155]

At the age of seventy-two, John Eliot, watching how King Philip's War destroyed everything he had built, including the Praying Towns, said, "I could do little, and yet I am determined through the grace of Christ never to retreat from work while I have the strength to move."[156]

William Carey said, "I can work. I can stand up to any difficulties. What I have achieved, I owe this to my character."[157]

In her book *From Jerusalem to Irian Jaya*, Ruth Tucker quotes Joanna Veenstra (the first missionary of the Christian Reformed Church to go to Nigeria):

> I took one trek through the hills, walking from place to place for
> nine days . . . We planned to stay over Sunday at a certain village
> but it proved that we were not welcome. They did not want to
> provide food for the carriers and the others who were with me.
> So they suffered a good deal of hunger. Rain hindered the people
> coming to meetings. I sat at a hut door, with an umbrella to keep
> me dry, while the people were huddled together inside the hut
> about a fire. On Sunday afternoon a heavy thunderstorm arose.
> The rain came down in torrents. The hut where I camped was a

154  "Twenty–Two Questions For John Catsimatidis," Forbes.com, October 1, 2009, https://www.forbes.com/2009/10/01/self-made-secrets-2009-entrepreneurs-management-catsimatidis.html#78ace2622817.

155  Charles Spurgeon, "On Necessity of Ministerial Progress," Chapter 2 in *Lectures to My Students*, Volume 3, 1996.

156  Ruth.A. Tucker, *From Jerusalem to Iranian Jaya: A Biographical History of Christian Missions* (Grand Rapids: Zondervan Academic, 2004).

157  Ibid.

grass-walled one, and the rain came rushing in until the whole place was flooded . . . Early the next morning we started off for a long walk to another hill . . . [158]

Martin Luther, hiding from the pope and the emperor and not being able to engage in teaching, translated the Bible into German. John Wesley rode seventy-five hundred kilometers (forty-six hundred miles) on horseback every year, and at that time, the country's main roads were like current country dirt roads. It was not by chance that he was called the "The Lord's Horseman." He stopped several times a day and preached to all those who wanted to listen. "I looked at the whole world as my parish. By this I mean that wherever I am, I considered it my indispensable duty to announce to everyone who wished to listen the joyful message of salvation."[159]

In his *Lectures on Revivals*, Charles G. Finney appeals to believers:

> "Why has generation after generation gone to hell while the Church has been dreaming and waiting for God to save them . . . And yet some people are terribly alarmed at all direct efforts to promote a revival, and they cry out: "You are trying to get up a revival in your own strength. Take care, you are interfering with the Sovereignty of God. Better keep along in the usual course, and let God bring a revival when He thinks it is best. God is a Sovereign, and it is very wrong for you to attempt to get up a revival, just because you think a revival is needed." This is just such preaching as the devil wants. And men cannot do the devil's work more effectually than by preaching up the Sovereignty of God as a reason why we should not put forth efforts to produce a revival.[160]

Jonathan Edwards spent thirteen hours in his office every day. When C. S. Lewis began the *Chronicles of Narnia* series, he wrote one book a year: *The Lion,*

---

158   Ibid.

159   Tony Lane, *A Concise History of Christian Thought* (Ada: Baker Academic, Revised Edition 2006).

160   Charles J. Finney, *Lectures on Revivals of Religion* (Torquay & Newton Abbott County Court: Diggory Press, 2007).

the Witch and the Wardrobe (1950); *Prince Caspian* (1951); *The Voyage of the Dawn Treader* (1952); *The Silver Chair* (1953); *The Horse and His Boy* (1954); *The Magician's Nephew* (1955); *The Last Battle* (1956). This was in addition to his other stories, essays, and teaching. He was over fifty years old.

Paul, defending his credentials as an apostle, writes, "To this very hour we go hungry and thirsty, we are in rags, we are brutally treated, we are homeless. We work hard with our own hands. When we are cursed, we bless; when we are persecuted, we endure it; when we are slandered, we answer kindly. We have become the scum of the earth, the garbage of the world—right up to this moment."[161]

Mark 1:35 says, "Very early in the morning, while it was still dark, Jesus got up, left the house and went off to a solitary place, where he prayed." Why did the Lord have to get up early for prayer? Because His day was filled with events. He instructed the disciples, preached to the masses, healed the sick, cast out demons, led theological debates with the scribes and Sadducees, and fed the needy.

There is a popular saying in evangelical circles, which I previously considered very spiritual: "When you don't have time and can only do one thing—either act or pray—it's better to pray." I now think these words are not entirely biblical; they don't reflect the spirit of Scripture. Scripture never divides a prayer from action. Jesus even has prayers that grow into action: "Truly I tell you, if anyone says to this mountain, 'Go, throw yourself into the sea,' and does not doubt in their heart but believes that what they say will happen, it will be done for them."[162]

What do you think would happen if Jesus had not died on the cross? What if He wanted it, talked about it, prayed for it, thirsted for it, but actually did not die on the cross? We would not receive salvation. Everything—all the sermons of the apostle Paul, Martin Luther's Ninety-five Theses, Augustine's books, William Carey's missionary work, Livingstone's research work, all the seminaries, all the churches, all the ministries, everything—would be useless.

---

161  1 Corinthians 4:11-13
162  Mark 11:23

When we detach action from the spiritual life, it's as if an unemployed person spends a year asking God for a job but only goes to one interview. I witnessed incidents when believers prayed for a long time for God to send evangelists or missionaries to their neighbors. When I hear this, I say, "Charles Spurgeon will not be resurrected, and there is no need to wait for missionaries from South Korea. We must preach the Gospel ourselves."

For missionaries, action often means to persevere in prayer, even when prayers are not answered, to continue witnessing when no one wants to listen, to invite people to your home when no one comes—all this when you catch yourself thinking that you have no idea what God is doing.

Once again, I want to say, you may not be able to evaluate the result, but you can evaluate the dedication.

## SHIELD OF FAITH

I like to think of a minister as a warrior. A warrior must be equipped when he goes to war. Paul discusses this topic in his letter to the Ephesians:

> Finally, be strong in the Lord and in his mighty power. Put on the full armor of God, so that you can take your stand against the devil's schemes. For our struggle is not against flesh and blood, but against the rulers, against the authorities, against the powers of this dark world and against the spiritual forces of evil in the heavenly realms. Therefore put on the full armor of God, so that when the day of evil comes, you may be able to stand your ground, and after you have done everything, to stand. Stand firm then, with the belt of truth buckled around your waist, with the breastplate of righteousness in place, and with your feet fitted with the readiness that comes from the gospel of peace. In addition to all this, take up the shield of faith, with which you can extinguish all the flaming arrows of the evil one. Take the helmet of salvation and the sword of the Spirit, which is the word of God.[163]

---

163 Ephesians 6:10-17

Let's pay attention to one important part of the armor: the shield of faith, which protects us from the arrows of the evil one. Before we employ our shield of faith, we must be sure of its reliability. Not all shields are suitable for war. Some shields may split in two when struck with a sword; others may be easily pierced by an arrow. Termites can destroy a wooden shield, and iron shields may rust. In the same way, one enemy in particular can undermine the strength of our Shield of Faith. This enemy is Doubt.

Doubt is not always bad. It's even necessary at times. Doubts are important in business and science.

Businessman Sheldon Adelson said in an interview, "I have been in business for 69 years, since I was 12 years old, and I came to learn, if you do things differently success will follow you like your shadow."[164] It is very important in business to subject products to questioning. For instance, if you have ever ironed your clothes, in the past, you may have had problems with the cord, but today you can buy a cordless iron.

This is even more important in science. Many scientists ask themselves the same question every day: Why do we do things the way we do? Some even go as far as questioning Newton's classical theory of gravity or the second law of thermodynamics.

Doubts and questions are also good for studying biblical texts or building a systematic theology. However, we begin to doubt the foundations of our faith, like the doctrine of the Trinity, the doctrine of the God-Man, salvation through faith), if we look at this not from the point of view of studying different approaches and the formation of new perspectives but rather as questioning our personal faith. If we say, "Is Jesus really God? Could God really be a man? Is it possible to believe the Bible as the Word of God?," then we move from the plane of critical analysis to the spiritual realm. It's quite easy to be knocked down on that slippery surface. We can lose the battle on

---

164  Evan Carmichael, "Sheldon Adelson's Top 10 Rules For Success," December 17, 2015, YouTube video, 0:55, https://www.youtube.com/watch?v=v2S8E7tFnk4.

this field because someone on this battlefield is strong and capable, and his only task is to destroy us.

In Central Asia, we highly honor Genghis Khan. Many books and articles have been written about his strategic skills. He sent undercover agents to study the location, weapons, organization, tactics, and mood of the enemy army. His spies acted under the guise of merchants and traders. For siege warfare, he recruited the best Chinese specialists and created a powerful engineering corps that was extremely effective, using various siege machines and catapults. One of his most-used tactics was taking the enemy by surprise. Mongolian cavalry could travel a long distance in a short time, each Mongolian taking two or three horses. Genghis Khan, like other commanders before him, used the tactic of the "weak link." When he saw that one of the enemy's flanks was weak in repulsing an attack, he focused his force on this area in order to break through the line and enter the enemy's rear, causing confusion.

The devil uses the same scheme. Doubt is a crack in our shield into which he is trying to insert a knife and then exploit that weakness as much as possible. You may ask yourself the question, "Is Jesus the only way to God?" Then the enemy offers other thoughts: "That's right. Aren't all religions the same? Of course, you can come to God in different ways. That's good thinking." The result is that you then have even more doubts to torment your soul.

If you look at the biblical texts, doubt is always shown in a negative light. Here are a few examples:

> In the morning, as they went along, they saw the fig tree withered from the roots. Peter remembered and said to Jesus, "Rabbi, look! The fig tree you cursed has withered!"
> "Have faith in God," Jesus answered. "Truly I tell you, if anyone says to this mountain, 'Go, throw yourself into the sea,' and does not doubt in their heart but believes that what they say will happen, it will be done for them. Therefore I tell you,

whatever you ask for in prayer, believe that you have received it, and it will be yours.[165]

If any of you lacks wisdom, you should ask God, who gives generously to all without finding fault, and it will be given to you. But when you ask, you must believe and not doubt, because the one who doubts is like a wave of the sea, blown and tossed by the wind. That person should not expect to receive anything from the Lord. Such a person is double-minded and unstable in all they do.[166]

"Lord, if it's you," Peter replied, "tell me to come to you on the water."

"Come," he said.

Then Peter got down out of the boat, walked on the water and came toward Jesus. But when he saw the wind, he was afraid and, beginning to sink, cried out, "Lord, save me!"

Immediately Jesus reached out his hand and caught him. "You of little faith," he said, "why did you doubt?"[167]

Do not enter into a debate with the devil. We have a good example in Eve. She decided to enter into a theological dispute, and we all know how that ended. Remember, Jesus defended Himself only by the Word of God without entering into negotiation.

It's a misconception that doubts penetrate our soul on their own. That's not the way it is. We ourselves open the door for the first doubt. It's a conscious decision. Why do we do this, knowing that doubt will kill our soul? I can give one answer, though it is irrational; take it for what it is. Inside each of us lives Gollum, a character from *The Lord of the Rings*. The New Testament calls this our old man, and he has "the Precious." I should note that he has a lot of things called Precious, but this is one of his favorites. Gollum has an irrational passion for the ring. The ring does not give him any strength or power—like an Aladdin

---

165   Mark 11:20-23
166   James 1:5-8
167   Matthew 14:28-31

lamp that makes wishes or boots that make you walk fast. It disfigures him. But despite all this, he is ready to give everything for the ring.[168]

Just so, our old man consciously makes a decision and opens wide the door allowing in the first doubt. When that doubt has worked its way into our soul, it plants seeds, and they sprout. The only right decision is never to open the door in the first place.

Once, I was trying to start a church in Northern Kazakhstan and found myself in the middle of spiritual warfare. I told my friend Anatoly, the pastor of a Pentecostal church, that I had many doubts, even though I wanted nothing to do with them. I wanted to get rid of them; they were killing me. He gave me good advice: "You cannot keep crows from flying above your head, but you can prevent them nesting in your hair." The wrong decision is to let them in and only then try to fight them. Which is just what I had done before.

Why I am talking about doubt? I believe doubt is the chief weapon the devil uses against any missionary. When you move from your home country (for example, the USA) to the field (for example, Egypt), you are not merely moving from one geographical location to another. Yes, you have left behind big retail stores with low prices, nice recreational centers, a good police system, and clean water. More importantly, you have left behind your large church, your home group, your pastor, and your dear neighborhood. You are moving from one spiritual location to another. As a missionary, you will find yourself in many unfamiliar situations. For instance, say you share the Gospel with a nice, young man at a men's club in Cairo, and he accepts with his whole heart. The next day, you intend to invite him to church, only to find out that he's in the hospital—his oldest brother broke his jaw because he put his faith in Jesus. Believe me, in the evening, the devil will come knocking on your door and say, "What did you do to this young man? Is this the abundant life you promised him? When his parents come to you, what you will say to

---

168 *The Lord of Rings* (film series), directed by Peter Jackson, Burbank, CA: New Line Cinema, 2001-2003.

them? Come on, don't you think Hell and Heaven are not readily apparent and, really, nobody knows exactly what happens after this life?"

Or say you have served faithfully for years and see almost no fruit in your ministry. You have another "knock" with new questions: "Who do you think you are? I told you to stay at home, work as an engineer. Do you believe Almighty God is concerned about your problems? Help will never come."

This is the devil's plan—to put a grain of doubt in your heart. If you open your heart to that doubt, this battle will rage inside of you, and you'll no longer be effective on the outside. You won't lose faith, but you'll no longer be fit for war. Such warriors are best left at home, or if they are admitted into the army, they are not very efficient and most often perish. A doubting evangelist is unlikely to convey the Gospel to anyone. A missionary who does not believe in his mission will not go the distance.

The question becomes, how shall we drive the enemy away? It's not a matter of trying to "hypnotize" or steady our faith. Actually, this is not about faith at all. We must go to the very root of our faith. When the enemy tries to create doubt about our faith, he wants to shake our knowledge of Who God is. The only weapon we have—and Jesus gave us a great example in the desert—is God's Word. Only a true, full, and authentic knowledge of the character and nature of our Father will defeat doubt.

The devil says, "You have been abandoned." God says, "Do not fear, for I am with you; do not be dismayed, for I am your God. I will strengthen you and help you; I will uphold you with my righteous right hand."[169]

The devil says, "Who are you?" God says, "You are a chosen people, a royal priesthood, a holy nation, God's special possession, that you may declare the praises of him who called you out of darkness into his wonderful light."[170]

The devil says, "Is God really good?" God says, "You are good, and what you do is good; teach me your decrees."[171]

---

169  Isaiah 41:10
170  1 Peter 2:9
171  Psalm 119:68

We must be certain of Who He is. We have to be sure in His Word. Perhaps that is why it is difficult some times for some of us with serious theological training to convey a simple Gospel message to those who need it. We might have four views of salvation, six theories about Hell, and five methods of evangelism, yet the worst thing is that we are not completely sure about anything.

CHAPTER 12

# WORKERS ON THE HOME FRONT

DURING A WAR, MEN GO to the front. Those who remain at home are often women, the elderly, children, and people with disabilities. To help in ways that they are able, women may grow wheat and potatoes; children may help in factories by packing cartridges in boxes; people with disabilities may manage farms. They work until blood comes from under their nails, and they drink water from puddles. When the war ends, the heroes of the front are called veterans, and those who helped at home are called home front workers.

To participate in the God's great global missionary movement, you need not go to the front yourself. You can be a missionary without leaving your home.

## PRAYER

In *The Celebration of Discipline*, Richard Foster quotes the words of Juliana of Norwich, "I am the ground of your praying. First, it is my will that you should have this; then I make it your will, too: then I make you ask for it, and you do so. How then should you not have what you pray for?"[172]

You can pray from the comfort of your home. This is your "wheat, ammunition, and medicine" for the front. Prayer overcomes great distances, ringing out in one world and being heard in another. It can change the history of the world and achieve the impossible.

The Prophet Isaiah came to the sick Hezekiah and said, "'This is what the LORD says: Put your house in order, because you are going to die; you

---

172 Richard J. Foster, *Celebration of Discipline: The Path to Spiritual Growth*, (San Francisco: Harper, 2000).

will not recover.' Hezekiah turned his face to the wall and prayed to the LORD, 'Remember, LORD, how I have walked before you faithfully and with wholehearted devotion and have done what is good in your eyes.'"[173] God heard the prayer of Hezekiah, saw the tears, and gave him fifteen more years of life; and He delivered him from the king of Assyria. In seminary, didn't they teach us that if a prophet says something, it will come true? Yet, how could God change His will?

The other day, I watched a 1961 Soviet newsreel called *Let Life Triumph*. The announcer said:

> How wonderful is the life of the Soviet people! But life has enemies; there on the outskirts of the city lies a nest of religious fanatics—obscurantists and haters of all living things. Members of an underground Christian sect of the evangelical faith went to their secret gatherings here. Shutting the doors and closing the windows tightly, the leaders of the sectarians for many hours, sometimes from dusk until dawn, tortured the minds and souls of deceived people and drove them to frenzy and seizures. And now, all this has come to an end. The trial of the leaders lasted for six days.

And now, the church elder Nikolai Egorov comes to the microphone: "In 1946, God in his great mercy, revealed Himself to me as the great creator and savior. Through the sacrifice of Jesus Christ, and through His blood shed on the cross, my sins are forgiven, and I fell in love with the Lord and gave myself to serve Him."

Brother Nikolay's speech was accompanied by loud, derisive laughter coming from communists attending the trial. Then the announcer continued "Dozens of people got their heads stuffed with such nonsense. But the truth cannot be hidden. Young girls deceived by the obscurantists were once cheerful and joyful. They have forgotten how to rejoice, they have forgotten

---

173  2 Kings 20:1-3

how to see the sun, they have been deceived. Look around and see how wonderful this world is."

The announcer ends with the words, "The obscurantists are condemned, but their victims live among us, and we are obliged to help them get out of darkness and gloom. Let life triumph!"[174]

The announcer didn't mention that "those who love life and see the sun" shot Vsevolod Meyerhold, the theater director and theorist of grotesque theater. Nikolay Vavilov, a great biologist, member of the Academy in Prague and Edinburgh and member of the Royal Society of London, died of starvation in prison and was buried in a common grave. The great twentieth century Russian poet Osip Mandelstam died in a Soviet transit camp. About 5.5 million people were repressed from 1921 to 1953. The number of victims in the U.S.S.R. alone is twenty million.

Hollywood grew up on the acting system of Konstantin Stanislavski because students of the master had fled the U.S.S.R. and introduced America to his name and the works of his Moscow Art Theater. "The Great Bass" singer Feodor Chaliapin left Bolshevik Russia, for the USA in 1922 and never returned. Mikhail Baryshnikov, considered by many to be the greatest ballet dancer of the twentieth century, defected in 1974 while on tour with the Bolshoi Ballet Theater in Canada.

In Kazakhstan, the communists labeled all the Kazakhs as *bai*[175] and seized all their possessions and at the same time resolved to make the nomads sedentary. People's cattle were taken and slaughtered on the spot. People would go outside and die. At the beginning of the twentieth century, Kazakhs engaged only in cattle breeding; there were no factories or plants, no farms growing wheat or tomatoes. From 1931 until 1933, two million people died in Kazakhstan. Only the Holocaust can be compared with this tragedy. What other people lost forty percent of their population? This did not happen

---

174 N Surovcev, *Let Life Triumph*, No. 26, directed by Ya. Volovik (1961, Newsreel Lower Volga Region), video.
175 Kazakh word for a rich man

in the second or fourth century; it happened in the twentieth century—the century of scientific and technological progress.

The Soviet Union lasted just seventy years, relatively few if viewed in terms of world history. The Roman Empire existed for five hundred years, the Ottoman Empire for 623 years. Some people say that the U.S.S.R. collapsed due to the shortcomings of a planned economy; some thank the coordinated work of Western intelligence agencies; some give credit to the fall in oil prices. However, there is a weightier reason: prayer—the simple and faithful prayers of the righteous.

Once, we were guests of believers in the USA. We met a grandmother who asked, "Where are you from?"

"From Kazakhstan," I replied.

"Where is that?"

"This is part of the former Soviet Union."

"Ah, I prayed for the Soviet Union." And then she went to prepare the table.

I would not be surprised if she prayed for the U.S.S.R. before I was born. Therefore, when you look at the magnet saying, "Pray for China" on your fridge and then pray, do not think that nothing is happening.

Mother Teresa said, "God shapes the world through prayer. The more prayers in the world, the better the world becomes, the greater the forces against evil."

## DONATION

Once, a pastor presented a beauty contest at the beginning of the church service. On the stage, sisters displayed different clothes. However, the clothes did not look at all like the latest fashions; they were worn, torn, and ridiculous with mismatched shoes. After the fashion show, the pastor stood behind the pulpit and said, "You probably wonder why our service is so unusual today and where these clothes come from. These are clothes that we collected last week to give to the poor. After we started sorting everything, I realized that

I was ashamed to give it to anyone. So now, I will preach a sermon, and next week we will collect clothes again."

When God gave the commandment to Moses about offerings, He said to give as an offering from your "firstfruits."[176] Why from "firstfruits?" Because the last fruits have rotted, been eaten by worms, or dried up. Such is the sinful nature of man; it's easier for us to part with what we do not need.

When you donate to a mission or a ministry, donate from the "firstfruits"—sacrifice as for the Lord. Suppose I am a believer, live in a house worth a million dollars, drive the latest BMW, fly first class, and support three missionaries for twenty dollars. In my opinion, this is not a donation; this is alms.

Just as a university student abandons a career as a Boeing engineer and in obedience to the Holy Spirit takes a "step of faith" to become a missionary in Angola, so, too, can you take a "step of faith" without leaving the comfort of your home. Give generously. When you give to another person sincerely from the heart, you give a part of yourself; you welcome that person into your world. When something that once belonged to you now belongs to another person, in a way, you say that you are one family. You're like a sister who can borrow her brother's sweatshirt.

When you give, don't look around, comparing yourself to others, asking, "Are others giving? How much are they giving? To whom are they giving?" Remember the words of Jesus to Peter: "What is that to you? You must follow me."[177]

Don't humiliate those who ask for support. When a missionary calls and asks for a meeting, you know exactly what the meeting will be about. "Simply let your 'Yes' be 'Yes,' and your 'No,' 'No.'"[178] If you aren't able to meet, be honest. Do not ask them to call you back tomorrow, or better still, after the weekend. Don't set an appointment and then cancel. Do not make them pursue you. If you humiliate the servant, you humiliate the Master. When you give, say two things: 1) Receive it from the Lord, and 2) You owe me nothing.

---

176  Leviticus 2:14
177  John 21:22b
178  Matthew 5:37 (BSB)

When you host a family of missionaries in your living room, look to the Lord. For Jesus says, "I was hungry and you gave me something to eat, I was thirsty and you gave me something to drink, I was a stranger and you invited me in, I needed clothes and you clothed me, I was sick and you looked after me, I was in prison and you came to visit me."[179]

Then, when you come to Him in His Kingdom, He will remember the time you and He had coffee in your living room.

## HELP

*Apollo 13* was to be the third spacecraft to go to the moon. However, after two days on the approach to the target, an accident occurred which not only put an end to landing on the moon, but also made it almost impossible to return to Earth. The mission control center created a team to oversee the rescue operation. They had to solve two problems: ensure the continued operation of the ship and work out an option for returning to the Earth, and all this had to be done at a great distance. Imagine that you are a flight control center and you have astronauts somewhere far off. How can you help them?

Ask yourself: what can I do that others cannot, or, what do I have that others do not? Do not succumb to the delusion, "Nobody needs what I have to offer."

One of the first trainings I developed and have since taught for many years is public speaking. This topic fascinated me after reading the book by Dale Carnegie, *How to Develop Self-Confidence and Influence People by Public Speaking*. Since then, I have tried to read everything I could find on the topic, while also studying the sermons of Haddon Robinson and Bill Hybels, the seminars of Les Brown and Jim Rohn, and speeches by Abraham Lincoln and Winston Churchill. I studied public speaking skills so much that I came to the conclusion that nobody needs what I would offer; everyone already knows everything on this particular theme. I thought others were like me.

179  Matthew 25:35-36

I felt this way until I began attending presentations by medical representatives speaking about the benefits of our products. For the first time, I saw senior medical personnel who, though they had no problems seeing patients, would sweat, blush, and shake when they stood in front of an audience. Doctors with years of experience put their colleagues to sleep much more efficiently than morphine. Brilliant medical students read a PowerPoint presentation word for word, exactly as the brand manager had given them. "Goodbye" was written on the last slide and they said, "Goodbye."

I started teaching "Business Presentation Skills for Medical Representatives," where I taught them how to grab attention at the start, how to introduce a topic and make an effective conclusion. I trained them to employ various approaches in presentations, how to use humor and tragedy, how to create key expressions, how to use "acting skills," and how to discern the audience's level of training. I also taught them how to use eye contact, facial expressions, and gestures. In addition, I showed examples of good public speaking: Martin Luther King, Ronald Reagan, Bill Clinton, Chuck Swindoll, Vladimir Putin, Patrick Lencioni, Andrei Mironov, and Gabriel Iglesias. Everyone enjoyed the training, but nothing changed in their next presentation.

When I spoke frankly with the employees, they said, "Kanat, public speaking skills are good for politicians during election campaigns and vice presidents during business lunches, but it doesn't work when promoting antibiotics or cardio drugs. Medicine is too complicated and boring."

After I insisted that these tools could be used in the medical field, one of the reps said, "Okay. You show us an example, and we'll see about that." This was a great idea.

I decided to promote an allergy medication. At the end of the second day of training, I said, "For two days, I taught you public speaking skills. Now, I'm going to take one of the products that you want to promote, using the PowerPoint provided by your brand manager, and demonstrate how the tools of public speaking can be used in the presentation of a medical product."

As one of our regional managers said, this had the effect of a bombshell. Now no one could say that it doesn't work. Since then, medical representatives have been using introductions and conclusions, employing videos and anecdotes, talking about the history of disease treatment in the Middle Ages, and even performing skits. One medical rep said, "Now people come to my presentations because they really want to hear me, not because I feed them lunch." Things that I thought were obvious and unnecessary turned out to be very popular and effective.

Say you are a programmer, and it seems to you that programmers are everywhere. To you, finding a competent plumber is harder than finding a competent programmer, and is there nothing easier than creating an algorithm or testing software? How can you help? You can't! Your church has a professional website and a programmer working on it, and he is clearly not dumber than you.

Then, say, one day a group comes to your church and presents their ministry in Thailand. They help women who engage in prostitution find God and then learn a skill. They have a clothing factory, and they grow mangoes on a plantation. They ask for prayers, missionaries, and donations to buy sewing machines. You would like to support them financially, but you want to know more about their ministry. So, you ask for a link to their website, where you can see photos, videos, and learn about the history of their ministry. They say that they don't have a website, but they do have color brochures. Here you can offer your help, and to do this, you need not leave your beloved Michigan, learn Thai, or learn how to preach the Gospel to Buddhists. All you need to do is what you already do and love, and it will take just a couple of hours a week for three weeks.

Then, this is when your friend, a Methodist church member, invites you to go rollerblading. You respond that you can't because you're working on a project for a ministry. Having learned from you about the project in more detail, he asks you to let him know when you are finished, and he'll promote this site on social networks (after all, he is the coolest SMM specialist in Lansing).

Those trapped on *Apollo 13* survived because not only were astronauts in the command center but also engineers, scientists, manufacturing specialists, and NASA management. Each one contributed: some had the ability to think logically; some had the ability to make quick decisions; some had personal flight experience; some knew everything about the trim of the ship, some about the engine, some about the power supply of the ship; individual teams developed possible options for returning to Earth (with or without a flyby of the moon). Together, they did the impossible.

There are many more specialists in the command center of the Church than NASA had in April 1970. We have architects, programmers, surgeons, builders, mathematicians, teachers, marketers, cooks, farmers, businessmen, and writers. Do not think that God uses only missionaries, pastors, preachers, teachers, and evangelists. God will find a role for everyone.

In Central Asia, our seminaries were mostly attended by Bible school faculty, pastors, and missionaries, but one time a group of builders came and decided to build a porch for us. They did not know how to teach or to establish churches; they did not know how Dispensationalism differs from Covenant Theology or what the controversy between Martin Luther and Ulrich Zwingli was during the Marburg dispute. They were older people with large, leather belts, out of which stuck out the most bizarre tools. They came to serve during their holidays. They built a porch for us where we set up a ping pong table, which became the only entertainment for teachers and students. On Saturdays and Sundays, we covered the table with a tablecloth, made refreshments, preached the Gospel, and engaged in discipleship. After many years, I have forgotten many lectures on systematic theology, but I still remember that veranda and those men in worn t-shirts and leather work belts.

If you follow the story of *Apollo 13* in the film by the same name, there is a moment when the NASA management is trying to find Ken Mattingly, who didn't fly because he had rubella. Ken had turned off the TV, turned off the phone, and gone to bed. They sent a man to his house, who pulls him out of bed and explains the situation.[180]

Today, God comes to your house, wakes you up, and says, "Get up. Do not sleep. We need you. There are people (in Turkey, Belarus, Morocco) who need to return home."

"What do you think? If a man owns a hundred sheep, and one of them wanders away, will he not leave the ninety-nine on the hills and go to look for the one that wandered off?"[181]

180 *Apollo 13*, directed by Ron Howard, Universal City, CA: Universal Pictures, 1995
181 Matthew 18:12

# CHAPTER 13

# WHEN ALL IS SAID AND DONE

IT WAS 2009. I SAT at the Uzbek Partnership Conference in the suburbs of Minneapolis, listening to missionaries speaking. There is a joke in HR circles: "An employee never achieved such perfection as in the preparation of a resumé." By analogy, it can be said that missionaries never achieve such perfection as in the presentation of their ministry. If I didn't know better, I would have thought that this was not about Uzbekistan but about the Roman Empire in the time of the emperor Constantine. Then we went to a group discussion.

I told the speaking missionaries that the picture they presented was not correct. They all replied in words like, "You are mistaken; everything is exactly as we said." I did not argue and thought that after lunch, I would express my point of view.

When my time at the microphone came, I was already up from my chair, intending to go to the stage, and the organizers invited another speaker, one not on the list. I thought surely they would call me later, so I waited, until I heard, "Thank you all very much for your participation! This concludes our conference."

A week later, I received a letter in which the conference organizers apologized for not having enough time for all the participants to speak. In fact, I was the only participant who did not speak.

I still do not know whether this was an accident or planned. It's quite possible that someone asked the organizers to make a change in the schedule. Today, I no longer work in a mission, and there is no one to tell me what not to write or say. In this book, I have said everything I wanted to say at that conference.

I want this book to be understood correctly. Please do not think I'm saying that everything that missionaries do is bad. There is certainly more good than bad. Missions provides Bible education for free, buy buildings for churches, pay medical expenses for ministers. Many missionaries sacrifice very much. They exchange their big houses in Colorado for small apartments in Kyrgyzstan; they could have worked for Google but instead chose a job for the Lord. They put the Lord above their own desires. It is not only individuals who sacrifice, but also spouses and children. In leaving their home cultures, they give up their refrigerators and televisions; some give up their homes. Some give up their lives. A missionary gave me a Bible, and missionaries taught me how to study the Bible.

Once, we took a taxi home after church. My wife and daughter were discussing the service when the taxi driver asked me, "Are you a believer?"

"Yes," I replied.

"Do you know a missionary named Tom?"

"No."

"He saved my life twice."

Intrigued, I asked, "How so?"

"I went camping with the church and fell into the river. I could not swim, and Tom jumped into the water and saved me. Later, when I had problems with alcohol, he paid for the rehabilitation center for me."

This man stopped going to church but still remembers the missionaries warmly.

It is quite possible to write a book about the good that missionaries have done in Kazakhstan or Morocco, but it's not necessary. This is declared at conferences and sent in mailings; you can read about it in *Christianity Today*. I wanted to talk about the other side. Few people talk about this because it is not very "fun"; they can be fired for it, and it frightens the heads of missions and key sponsors.

But talking about this topic is very important. In all large companies or international organizations, the important question is asked, "What is one thing we could do better?" How can we improve our product? How can we better satisfy our customers? How can our non-profit organization better cooperate with the government?

What we do is more important than the production of a new medicine for hypertension or an alternative-fuel automobile. Today's problems in Syria, in Afghanistan, in the Middle East cannot be solved by air-to-surface missiles. "The Gospel is the power of God for the salvation of everyone who believes."[182]

When we meet with Christ in His Kingdom and see Him as He is, many of us will have regrets: "If I could go back, I would live differently. I would serve differently."

At the beginning of the book, I mentioned my grandmother, who taught me how to pray. She lived with us; my parents worked, and she was like a mother to me. She taught me to read, count, have respect for elders, and have my own opinion. I loved her very much. Therefore, I shared the Gospel with her several times. She always listened attentively but was silent. In one of my visits home, I again decided to tell her again about Isa. She was already ninety years old; she didn't see or hear very well, so I had to shout. In the middle of my sermon, she took my hand and said, "I accepted your Prophet into my heart." When I went home, I left with peace because she always knew that for me, Isa was not just a prophet; and Muslims do not accept prophets into their hearts. A few months later, my father called me to tell me of the death of my grandmother. My father told me something else, something I did not know.

He said, "You know, when Mom was dying, I was sitting next to her, and a dove landed on the windowsill outside. I opened the window for more air"—my parents' apartment is on the second floor of a five-story building—"and Mother said, 'Do not chase him away.' I looked at my mother, then looked at the dove, but he was no longer there. When I looked back at my mother, she, too, was already gone."

---

182  Romans 1:16

Then Jesus came to them and said, "All authority in heaven and on earth has been given to me. Therefore go and make disciples of all nations, baptizing them in the name of the Father and of the Son and of the Holy Spirit, and teaching them to obey everything I have commanded you. And surely I am with you always, to the very end of the age."[183]

The Messenger died for the sake of the message. This message leads us home.

---

183  Matthew 28:18-20

# BIBLIOGRAPHY

Barclay, William. "Commentary on John 3." *William Barclay's Daily Study Bible.* https://www.studylight.org/commentaries/dsb/john-3.html, 1956-1959.

Benge, Janet and Geoff. *Count Zinzendorf: Firstfruit (Christian Heroes: Then & Now).* Edmonds: YWAM Publishing, 2006.

Blackaby, Henry. *Experiencing God: Knowing and Doing the Will of God.* Nashville: B&H Books, Revised Edition, 2008.

Calvin, John. *Institutes of the Christian Religion.* Aslan Publishing, 1997.

Currey, Mason. *Daily Rituals: How Artists Work.* New York City: Knopf, 2013.

Deere, Jack. *Surprised by the Power of the Spirit: Discovering How God Speaks and Heals Today.* Grand Rapids: Zondervan Academic, 1996.

Erasmus, Desiderious. *The Manual of a Christian Knight.* Kharkiv: Litera Nova Publishing. 2017.

Finney, Charles J. *Lectures on Revivals of Religion.* Torquay & Newton Abbott County Court: Diggory Press, 2007.

Foster, Richard J. *Celebration of Discipline: The Path to Spiritual Growth.* San Francisco: Harper, 2000.

Garrison, David. *Church Planting Movements: How God is Redeeming a Lost World.* Monument: WIGTake Resources LLC, 2004.

Lane, Tony. *A Concise History of Christian Thought*. Ada: Baker Academic, Revised Edition 2006.

Moo, Douglas J. *The Epistle to the Romans*. Grand Rapids: Wm. B. Eerdmans Publishing Co., 1996.

Parandowski, Jan. *Alchemy of the Word*. Moscow: Progress Publishing, 1972.

Silver, Yitzchak. *Paths of Peace and Goodness*. Eds. Zvi Wasserman and Leia Shukhman. Russia, 2012.

Spurgeon, Charles. "On Necessity of Ministerial Progress." Chapter 2 in Lectures to My Students. Volume 3. 1996.

St. Augustine. *Confessions*. Metairie: Renaissance Publishing, 1991.

St. Gregory the Theologian. "To His Soul." In Spiritual Creations, Instructing the Basics of Life. Ark Publishing, 2000.

Steinbeck, John. *The Grapes of Wrath*. New York City: Viking, 1939.

Swanky, Shawn. *How to Improve Your Movie Literacy with Akira Kurosawa*. Morrisville: Lulu.com, 2016.

Tozer, A.W. *The Pursuit of God*. Tustin: Loki's Publishing, 2017.

Tucker, Ruth A. *From Jerusalem to Iranian Jaya: A Biographical History of Christian Missions*. Grand Rapids: Zondervan Academic, 2004.

Warren, Rick. *The Purpose Driven Church: Every Church is Big in God's Eyes*. Grand Rapids: Zondervan, 1995.

Wilde, Oscar. *The Star-Child*. Edinburgh: Floris Books, 1999.

# ABOUT THE AUTHOR

KANAT YESMAGAMBETOV IS A PREACHER and minister. For many years, Kanat taught subjects such as "Bible Study Methods," "Narration and Poetry," "Homiletics," and "Church History" at a Bible school. Kanat is currently serving as a teaching elder in a local Evangelical church and is the founder of *Called* ministry. Kanat lives with his family in Almaty, Kazakhstan.

For more information about
Kanat Yesmagambetov
and

*What is Wrong with Western Missions?*
please visit:

www.called.website

# More from Ambassador International

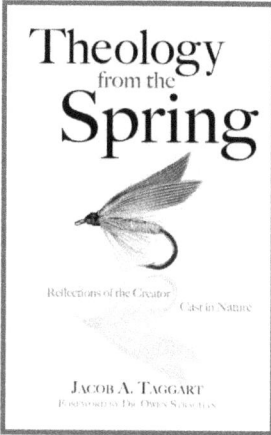

## Theology from the Spring

Reflections of the Creator Cast in Nature

JACOB A. TAGGART

Through vignettes of fresh water springs and fly fishing analogies, *Theology From the Spring* provides the reader with eyes for seeing how God's creation—the natural world—can provide answers to the oldest divine mystery and make sense of the beauty and chaos we see within the created order.

Join Christine Paxson and Rose Spiller as they explore the answers to these and many other questions about the true Gospel message in *No Half-Truths Allowed: Understanding the Complete Gospel Message*. Learn what Jesus did for you, why He did it, and how you can articulate the Gospel to others.

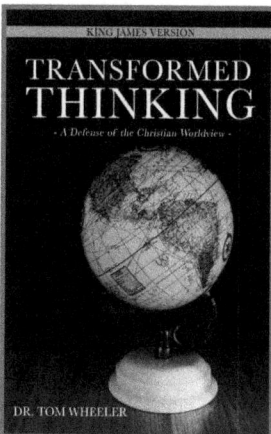

## NO half-truths ALLOWED

UNDERSTANDING THE COMPLETE GOSPEL MESSAGE

CHRISTINE PAXSON & ROSE SPILLER

## KING JAMES VERSION

### TRANSFORMED THINKING

*A Defense of the Christian Worldview*

DR. TOM WHEELER

In *Transformed Thinking*, Tom Wheeler clearly lays out the most fundamental beliefs of Christianity and compares them to other worldviews, providing arguments to support his beliefs. Even though this book is purposed for the classroom setting, it would be a beneficial read for any believer who wants to have a firm foundation on which to share their beliefs with unbelievers.

www.ingramcontent.com/pod-product-compliance
Lightning Source LLC
Chambersburg PA
CBHW071437090426
42737CB00011B/1683